Conversations / Konversationen in Haarlem

Kate Pelling

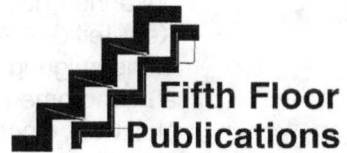
Fifth Floor Publications

Conversations in Haarlem
By Kate Pelling

Published by Fifth Floor Publications, London,
UK and Frankfurt am Main, Germany

Copyright 2020 Fifth Floor Publications and
Kate Pelling

ISBN **978-0-9576128-3-9**

Konversationen in Haarlem
von Kate Pelling

Verlegt durch Fifth Floor Publications, London,
Großbritannien und Frankfurt am Main,
Deutschland

Copyright 2020 Fifth Floor Publications und
Kate Pelling

ISBN **978-0-9576128-3-9**

Contents / Inhaltsverzeichnis:

Introduction

Conversations in Haarlem is a series of drawings that I made in Haarlem, Netherlands, on the 26th December 2018. The drawings show ordinary people going about their daily lives, walking down Korte Veerstraat, along Spaarne or through Grote Markt, some are waiting for a bus, some are walking slowly and taking in their surroundings, and others are moving faster because there is somewhere that they need to be.

I saw many people in Haarlem that day, but I went there to talk to Hendrick...

Hendrick Goltzius (1558-1617) was an artist, specifically a printmaker, draughtsman and painter, who was born in Mulbracht in North Rhine-Westphalia, Germany. Goltzius began to study engraving with Dirck Volckertszoon Coornhert (1522-1590) in Kleve, also in North Rhine-Westphalia, and when he was nineteen years old he and Coornhert moved to Haarlem in the Netherlands. Goltzius lived and worked in Haarlem for the rest of his life.

Early in 2018, I came across some of Goltzius's engravings in the Städel Museum in Frankfurt am Main, Germany. According to A. Hyatt Mayor, Goltzius 'was the last professional engraver who drew with the authority of a good painter and the last who invented many pictures for others to copy' (1971, p. 421). I began to draw four of Goltzius's engravings: *The Four Disgracers: Icarus, Phaeton, Tantalus, and Ixion* (1588). In these engravings, four figures are shown

Einleitung

Konversationen in Haarlem ist eine Serie von Zeichnungen, die ich am 26. Dezember 2018 in Haarlem in den Niederlanden anfertigte. Diese Zeichnungen zeigen ganz gewöhnliche Menschen, die ihren täglichen Aktivitäten nachgehen. Einige gehen eine Straße wie die Korte Veerstraat oder die Spaarne entlang, andere durch den Grote Markt; manche warten auf einen Bus, andere laufen gemächlich und betrachten die Gegend, wieder andere bewegen sich schneller, da sie irgendwohin müssen.

An jenem Tag sah ich viele Menschen in Haarlem, aber ich war gekommen, um mit Hendrick zu sprechen ...

Hendrick Goltzius (1558-1617), geboren in Mulbracht in Nordrhein-Westfalen, Deutschland, war ein Künstler, vor allem ein Grafiker, Zeichner und Maler. Er erlernte zunächst die Kunst des Kupferstechens bei Dirck Volckertszoon Coornhert (1522-1590) in Kleve in Nordrhein-Westfalen. Als er neunzehn Jahre alt war, zogen er und Coornhert nach Haarlem in die Niederlande, wo er für den Rest seines Lebens lebte und arbeitete.

Anfang 2018 sah ich einige der von Goltzius gefertigten Kupferstiche im Städel Museum in Frankfurt am Main in Deutschland. Laut A. Hyatt Mayor war Goltzius "der letzte professionelle Kupferstecher, der mit der Autorität eines guten Malers zeichnete und der letzte, der viele Bilder schuf, die andere nachzeichnen" (1971, Seite 421). Ich begann damit, vier von Goltzius'

tumbling through the air. The figures are seen from unusual angles, twisted to maximise the number of tensed muscles so there are many examples of foreshortening, where a part of the body is reduced or distorted in order to convey the illusion of three-dimensional space as perceived by the human eye. Foreshortened limbs are challenging to draw, so the engravings show off Goltzius's skill as a draughtsman.

My intention was not to 'copy' the engravings as Mayor had suggested, and indeed my drawings look very different to Goltzius's. I wanted to examine them in my own way – to use drawing as a way of thinking through the works. I made approximately 100 drawings and during this process I considered how I would interpret the figures, and to begin to understand them and the context that they were made in. As I drew, a lot of questions came up that I wanted to talk to Goltzius about. Firstly, we would talk about life drawing and human anatomy, which I had also studied for many years. I spent hundreds of hours of learning to draw the human figure, but I was also employed as a life model for a number of years in colleges and for art groups across Merseyside, UK. As well as the first hand experience of drawing, I learnt from modelling because I was able to feel where a particular pose put stress on the muscles and how the weight of the body was distributed. I could then utilise these different perspectives within my drawing practice.

I would also talk to Goltzius about different aspects of being an artist. I would compare how our backgrounds have affected our respective work and careers. Goltzius was not from a rich

Werken zu zeichnen: *Vier Stürzende: Ikarus, Phaeton, Tantalus und Ixion* (1588). Sie zeigen vier Personen, die durch die Luft zu Boden stürzen. Ihre Körper werden aus ungewöhnlichen Blickwinkeln betrachtet und gedreht, um die Anzahl der angespannten Muskeln zu erhöhen. Es gibt hier viele Beispiele für perspektivische Verkürzung, wobei ein Teil des Körpers verkleinert oder verzerrt dargestellt wird, um dem Betrachter die Illusion eines dreidimensionalen Raumes zu bieten. Das Zeichnen von perspektivisch verkürzten Gliedmaßen ist stets eine Herausforderung und die Werke belegen eindrucksvoll Goltzius' zeichnerische Fähigkeiten.

Ich hatte nicht vor, die Darstellungen, wie von Mayor vorgeschlagen, nachzuzeichnen. In der Tat sehen meine Zeichnungen ganz anders aus als die von Goltzius. Meine Absicht war es, sie auf meine Art zu untersuchen - das Zeichnen als eine Art des Denkens durch die erstellten Werke einzusetzen. Ich fertigte ungefähr 100 Zeichnungen an und widmete mich bei diesem Prozess besonders dem Gedanken, wie ich die dargestellten Personen interpretieren würde. Dabei begann ich, sie und den Kontext, in dem sie geschaffen wurden, besser zu verstehen. Beim Zeichnen kamen mir viele Fragen, die ich Goltzius gerne stellen wollte, in den Sinn. Zuerst wollte ich mit ihm über die Darstellung von Lebewesen und die menschliche Anatomie sprechen, denen ich mich wie er viele Jahre gewidmet hatte. Ich habe hunderte Stunden damit verbracht, das Zeichnen des menschlichen Körpers zu erlernen, aber ich war auch selbst mehrere Jahre lang als Modell in Universitäten und für Kunstgruppen

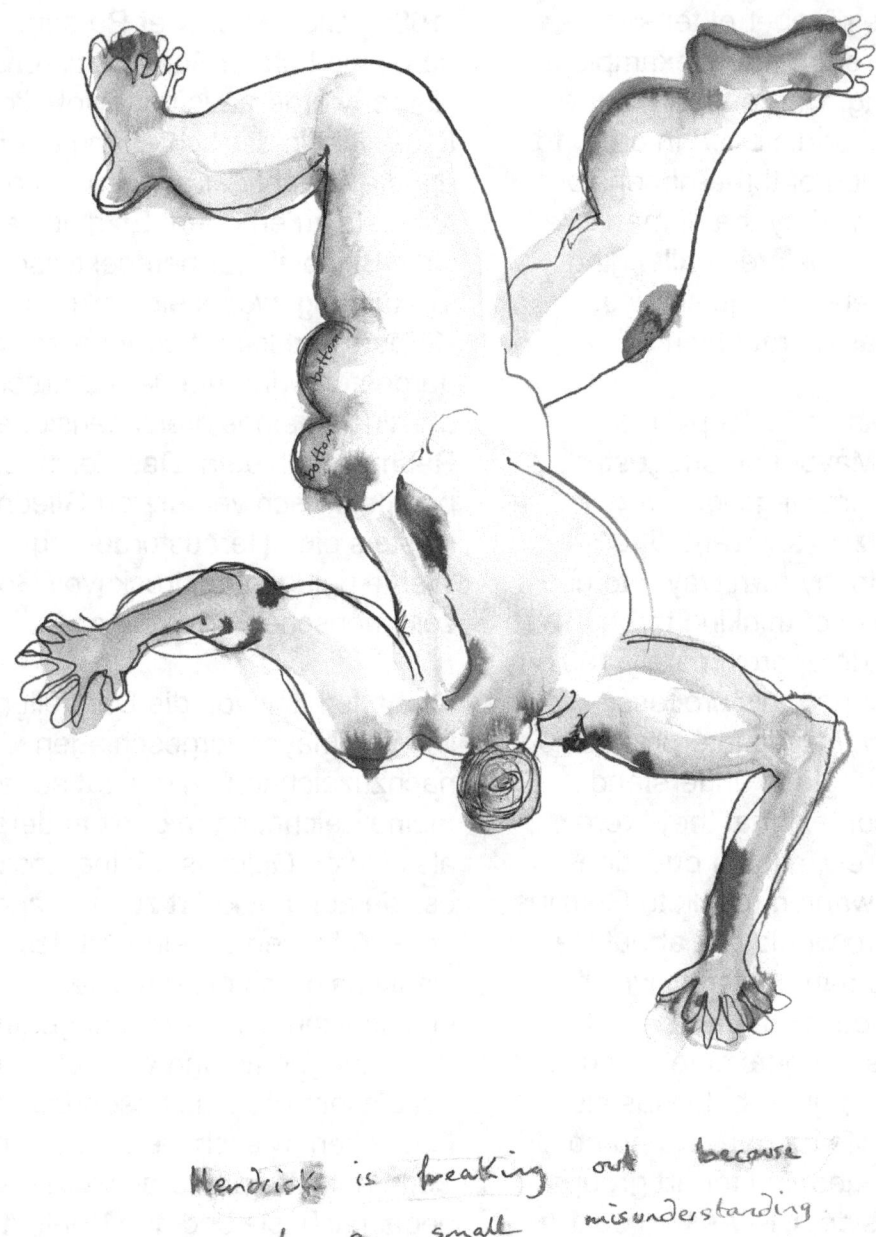

Hendrick is freaking out because of a small misunderstanding

24/06/2018

Image 1: *Conversations on Falling:*
Hendrick is freaking out because of a small
misunderstanding, 2018, ink on paper,
42 x 28.8 cm

Darstellung 1: *Konversationen über das Fallen:*
Hendrick wird wütend wegen eines kleinen
Missverständnisses, 2018, Tinte auf Papier,
42 x 28,8 cm

family and at the beginning of his career I imagine that he relied heavily on his connection with Coornhert, who was a writer, philosopher, translator, politician, theologian and artist, and is considered to be the father of Dutch Renaissance scholarship. I am from a working class family, and despite having a thorough education in visual art (18 years of study, culminating in a PhD from Chelsea College of Art, London, UK), I did not have a mentor as Goltzius did. I had no support systems, so most of my art education was on a part time basis and dominated by trying to earn enough money to live and to pay the tuition fees. As a result of this I have always felt held back – financially, socially and intellectually. Even though I am now living and working in Germany, where the cost of living is significantly cheaper than in the UK, the political and cultural baggage of being both working class and an artist remains ever-present.

At the age of 21, Goltzius married Mrs Matham – unfortunately, during my research I was unable to discover her full name and there are few details recorded of her life. However, it is documented that Matham was older than Goltzius and a widow, and her money enabled Goltzius to work independently in Haarlem. I have never married anyone, for money or otherwise, primarily because I have always been completely focussed on my work. If I had married for money like Goltzius did, I imagine that my life and work would have been very different, but it would be frivolous to imagine exactly how that would be.

I believe that Goltzius would be intrigued with the possibilities of making art in contemporary society. I

in Merseyside in Großbritannien tätig. So lernte ich gleichermaßen durch das Zeichnen und durch meine Tätigkeit als Modell, da ich selbst erlebte, wie und wo eine bestimmte Position Druck auf die Muskeln aufbaut und wie das Körpergewicht sich verteilt. Diese verschiedenen Erfahrungen konnte ich dann in meiner eigenen zeichnerischen Praxis nutzen.

Auch über verschiedene Aspekte des Lebens als Künstler wollte ich mit Goltzius sprechen und dabei vergleichen, wie unsere Herkunft unsere Tätigkeit und unseren Weg als Künstler beeinflusst hat. Er stammte nicht aus einer besonders wohlhabenden Familie und ich glaube, dass er zu Beginn seiner Karriere sehr auf die Verbindung zu Coornhert, der Autor, Philosoph, Übersetzer, Politiker, Theologe und Künstler war und als Vater der Renaissance in den Niederlanden gilt, angewiesen war. Ich stamme selbst aus einer Familie der Arbeiterschicht und obwohl ich eine fundierte Ausbildung in visueller Kunst habe (18 Jahre Studium, abgeschlossen mit dem Doktortitel des Chelsea College of Art in London), hatte ich im Gegensatz zu ihm keinen Mentor. Da ich kein Netzwerk von Unterstützern hatte, absolvierte ich den größten Teil meiner Studien in Teilzeit, stets konfrontiert mit der Notwendigkeit, genügend Geld zum Leben und zum Bezahlen der Studiengebühren zu verdienen. Daher fühlte ich immer starken Druck: finanziell, sozial und intellektuell. Obwohl ich nun in Deutschland, wo die Lebenshaltungskosten deutlich niedriger sind als in Großbritannien, lebe und arbeite, ist die politische und kulturelle Belastung, aus einer

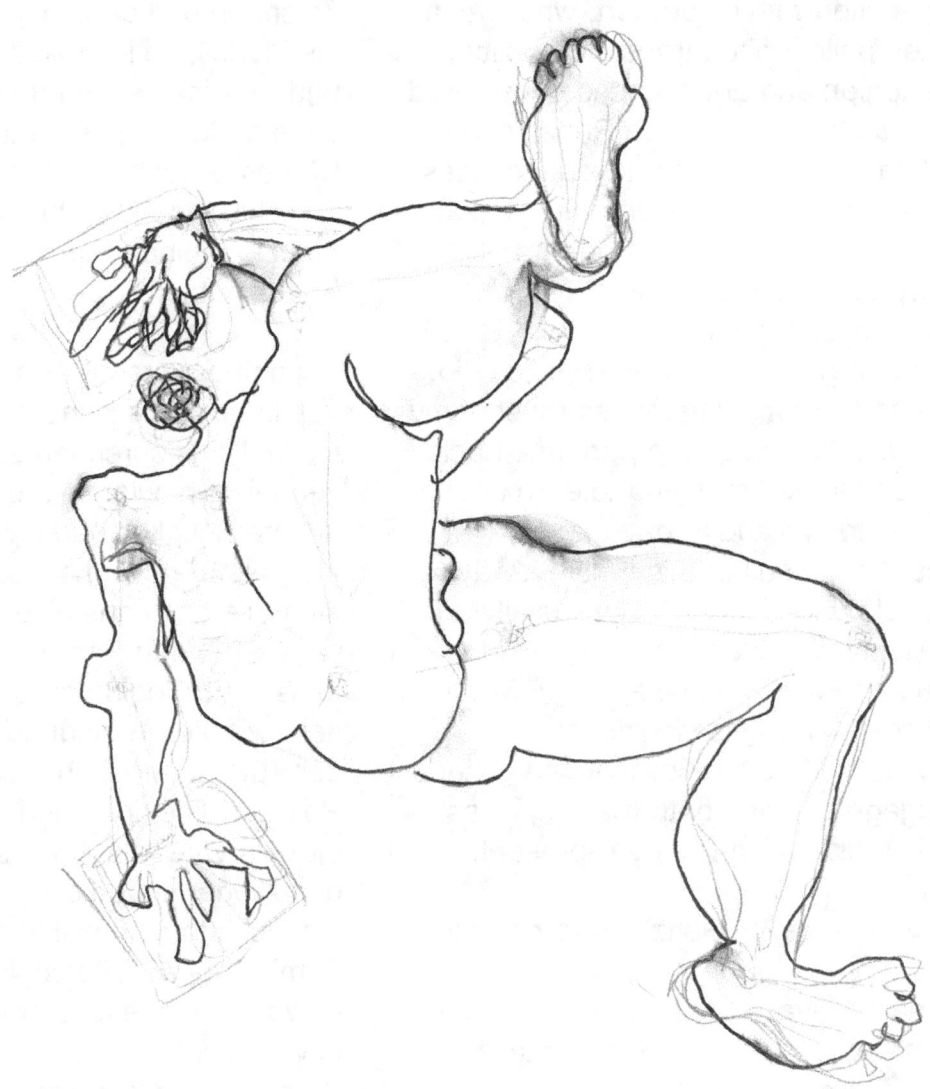

Hendrick engraves with his right
hand and draws with his left.
I can't afford to do engraving

07/10/2018

Image 2: *Conversations on Falling: Hendrick engraves with his right hand and draws with his left. I can't afford to do engraving*, 2018, ink and pencil on paper, 42 x 28.8 cm

Darstellung 2: *Konversationen über das Fallen: Hendrick sticht mit der rechten Hand und zeichnet mit der linken. Ich kann Kupferstechen nicht bieten*, 2018, Tinte und Bleistift auf Papier, 42 x 28,8 cm

am sure that he would have embraced modern technologies, for example the potential opened up by film and video, digital drawing techniques, and the proliferation of printmaking methods, both digital and analogue. Maybe we would have collaborated on a publication, or he might have appeared in one of my videos. But of course it was impossible for me to talk to him because he died hundreds of years ago. However, I felt that by this point in our relationship we would at least be on first name terms...

Prior to my trip to Haarlem, my drawings based on Hendrick's *The Four Disgracers* (1588) were titled *Conversations on Falling* (2018). In English there are many expressions that use 'falling', from literally 'falling from the sky', to idiomatic expressions, such as 'falling in love with someone' and 'falling out with someone'. My drawings of *The Four Disgracers* exploited the many forms of 'falling' as they traced conversations between myself and Hendrick (see Images 1, 2, 3 and 4). While working on these 'falling' drawings, I thought about Hendrick and our many similarities. Of course, the fact that we are both artists is the most obvious similarity, and even though life is quite different now compared to the 16th Century, the day to day work of maintaining a practice and the need to prioritise that over all other pursuits remains constant.

Another similarity is that Hendrick and I are both migrants. Hendrick moved from Germany to the Netherlands in 1577, and I moved from the UK to Germany in 2013. As I wrote in *[Video] Klappe* (2014):

Arbeiterfamilie zu kommen und dennoch Künstlerin zu sein, nach wie vor vorhanden.

Als er 21 Jahre alt war, heiratete Goltzius Frau Matham, deren vollständigen Namen ich leider bei meinen Nachforschungen nicht in Erfahrung bringen konnte, da nur wenige Einzelheiten über ihr Leben der Nachwelt überliefert wurden. Bekannt ist jedoch, dass sie älter als er und verwitwet war und dass ihre finanziellen Mittel ihm ein unabhängiges Schaffen in Haarlem ermöglichten. Ich selbst habe niemals geheiratet, weder aus finanziellen noch aus anderen Gründen, vor allem, weil ich mich immer voll auf meine Arbeit konzentriert habe. Wenn ich wie Goltzius wegen des Geldes geheiratet hätte, glaube ich, dass mein Leben und Schaffen ganz anders geworden wären, doch wäre es wohl leichtfertig, sich vorzustellen, wie genau das sein würde.

Meiner Meinung nach wäre Goltzius fasziniert von den vielfältigen Möglichkeiten, die unsere Gesellschaft heute den Kunstschaffenden bietet. Sicherlich hätten ihn moderne Techniken wie beispielsweise das Potenzial von Film, Video und digitalen Zeichentechniken sowie die heutigen Möglichkeiten der Grafikherstellung und des Drucks, sei es analog oder digital, begeistert. Vielleicht hätten wir zusammen ein Projekt konzipiert oder er wäre in einem meiner Videos zu sehen gewesen. Aber natürlich war es mir unmöglich, mit ihm zu sprechen, da er vor hunderten von Jahren gestorben ist. Dennoch hatte ich das Gefühl, dass wir zu diesem Zeitpunkt unserer

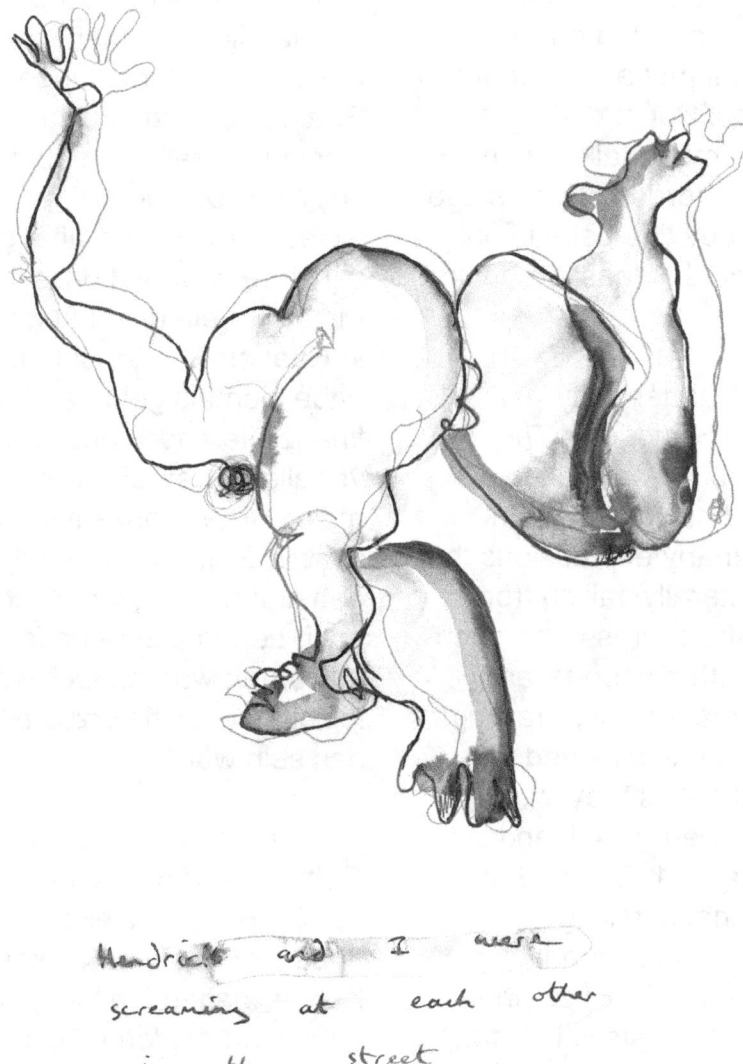

Hendrick and I were
screaming at each other
in the street

24/06/2018

Image 3: *Conversations on Falling: Hendrick and I were screaming at each other in the street*, 2018, ink and pencil on paper, 42 x 28.8 cm

Darstellung 3: *Konversationen über das Fallen: Hendrick und ich schreien einander auf der Straße an,* 2018, Tinte und Bleistift auf Papier, 42 x 28,8 cm

My primary motivation for wanting to leave London was the current political and cultural climate in the UK, which operates from a very narrow viewpoint and remains dominated by issues around class and hierarchy. I spent several years trying to live and work in London, but I found myself irrevocably inhibited by economic issues and excluded by the narrow cultural and social frameworks. I was unable to make significant progress in any direction, personally or professionally. I remember describing it at the time as beyond the cliché of hitting a glass ceiling, it was more like being encased in a small glass box that didn't allow me to stand up to my full height, let alone move up, down, sideways or backwards. Now that I am based permanently in Germany, I have considerably more room for manoeuvre. (2014, p. 8)

Since I wrote about my reasons for moving, the political situation in the UK has shifted further and further to the right and Brexit in particular has created extreme division in the country. I had benefitted from the freedom of movement related to being a citizen of the European Union and unfortunately now life is becoming considerably more complicated. Like Hendrick, who stayed in Haarlem for the rest of his life, I will never move back to the UK, it wouldn't be possible financially but more importantly it is not feasible from a personal, cultural or political perspective.

In addition to being an artist and a migrant, the most curious similarity between myself and Hendrick is that we are both ambidextrous. Hendrick burned his right hand in an accident

Beziehung zumindest damit beginnen sollten, einander zu duzen....

Vor meiner Reise nach Haarlem war der Titel meiner auf Hendricks *Vier Stürzende* (1588) basierenden Zeichnungen *Konversationen über das Fallen* (2018). In der englischen Sprache gibt es viele Kollokationen und Ausdrücke, die sich mit dem Begriff des Fallens bilden; vom sprichwörtlichen "zu Boden fallen" bis zu idiomatischen Redewendungen wie "sich in jemanden verlieben (falling in love with someone)" oder "sich mit jemandem streiten (falling out with someone)". Meine Zeichnungen der *Vier Stürzenden* beschäftigen sich mit den vielfältigen Bedeutungen des "Fallens" und nehmen Bezug auf Konversationen zwischen Hendrick und mir (Darstellung 1, 2, 3 und 4). Während der Arbeit an diesen Zeichnungen des "Fallens" dachte ich über Hendrick und unsere vielen Gemeinsamkeiten nach. Die offensichtlichste von ihnen ist freilich die Tatsache, dass wir beide Künstler sind. Obwohl das Leben heute sich von dem des sechzehnten Jahrhunderts deutlich unterscheidet, haben sich die tägliche Praxis des Künstlers und die damit einhergehende Notwendigkeit, dem künstlerischen Schaffen Priorität über alle anderen Lebensbereiche einzuräumen, nicht geändert.

Eine weitere Gemeinsamkeit ist, dass Hendrick und ich beide Migranten sind. Er zog 1577 aus Deutschland in die Niederlande; ich zog 2013 aus Großbritannien nach Deutschland. Wie ich in *[Video] Klappe* (2014) schrieb:

Meine vorrangige Motivation, London zu verlassen, war das aktuelle politische und kulturelle Klima in Großbritannien,

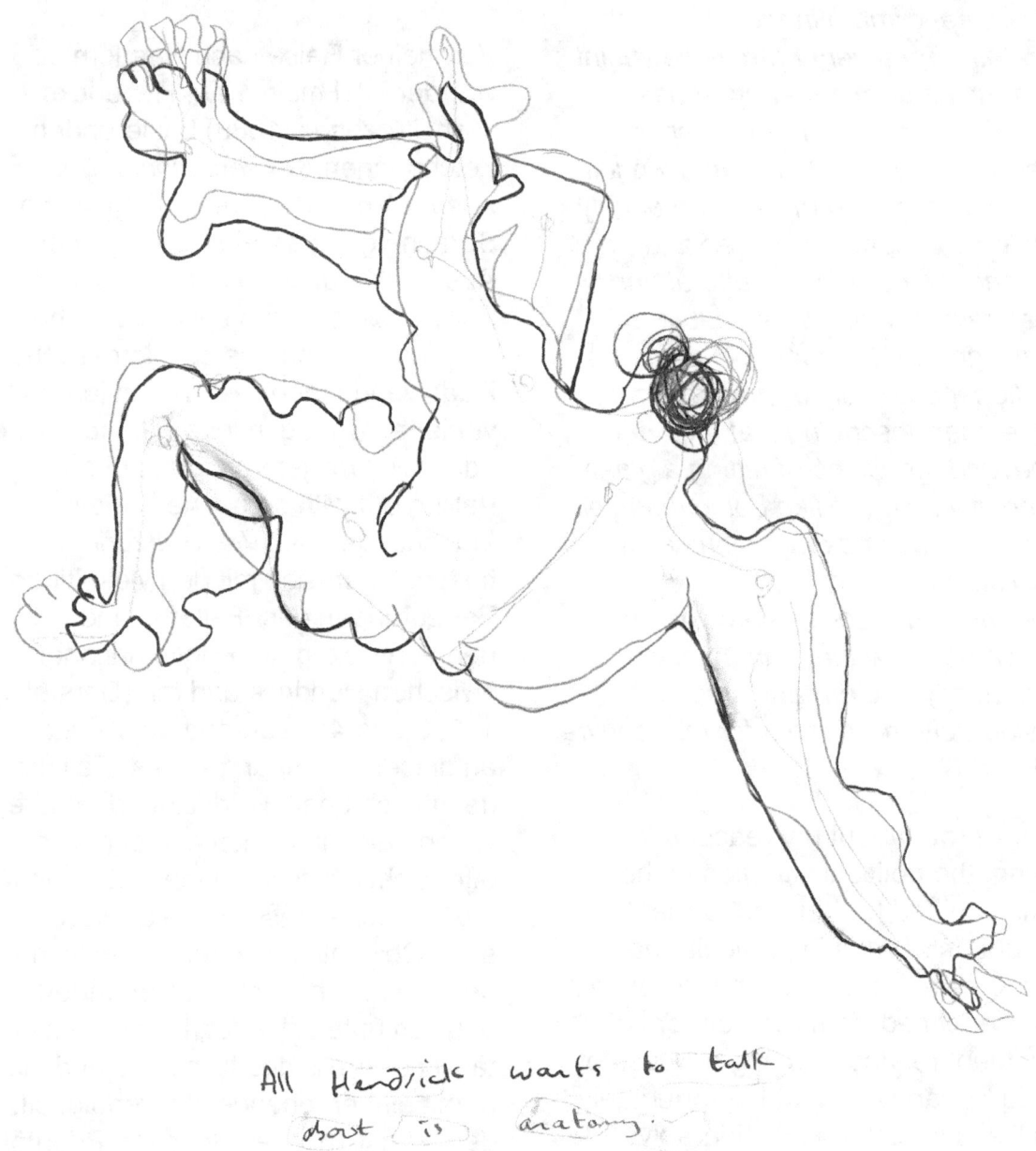

All Hendrick wants to talk
about is anatomy.

07/07/2018

Image 4: *Conversations on Falling: All Hendrick wants to talk about is anatomy*, 2018, ink and pencil on paper, 42 x 28.8 cm

Darstellung 4: *Konversationen über das Fallen: Hendrick will nur über Anatomie sprechen*, 2018, Tinte und Bleistift auf Papier, 42 x 28,8 cm

when he was very young – 'he had tumbled into a fire and cramped his right hand permanently shut' (Mayor, 1971, p. 419). As a result of this he was only able to hold the engraving tool in his right hand, using the muscles within his upper arm and shoulder to manipulate it. In a biography of Hendrick, Karel van Mander suggests that he engraved with his right hand and drew with his left hand (1604, p. 282). Evidence of this is a drawing of his right hand in the collection of Teylers Museum, Haarlem (see Image 5).

I discovered that I was ambidextrous in 1997 during a life drawing class in Liverpool, UK. A drawing exercise required us to use our 'other' hand and the drawings that I made that day were far superior to the ones I had been producing with my so-called 'dominant' hand. Since then I have alternated my hands when drawing, depending on what I wanted to achieve. My right hand can produce greater accuracy but my left hand produces a much more interesting line, as can be seen in drawings of my own hands (see Images 6 and 7).

I felt as if I had got to know Hendrick a little bit, and there were lots of things that I would talk to him about – so I understandably wanted to 'meet' him. Late in 2018, I planned a trip to Haarlem so that I could walk along the streets of the place where Hendrick had lived and worked. I travelled by train from my home in Niederbrechen, Germany, to Amsterdam and then on to Haarlem, but it soon became clear that Hendrick wasn't anywhere to be found... I am not sure exactly what I expected to see in Haarlem, but I felt the absence of Hendrick very strongly. This feeling

das eine sehr eingeschränkte Sichtweise einnimmt und weiterhin von gesellschaftlicher Herkunft und den damit verbundenen Hierarchien dominiert wird. Ich versuchte mehrere Jahre, in London zu leben und zu arbeiten und wurde doch immer wieder durch finanzielle Probleme und den überaus enggefassten kulturellen und sozialen Rahmen ausgeschlossen und in meinem Schaffen behindert. In keinem Bereich, weder persönlich noch beruflich, konnte ich deutliche Fortschritte erzielen. Ich erinnere mich daran, dass ich die Situation damals als über die Vorstellung der in der englischen Sprache sprichwörtlichen gläsernen Zimmerdecke, bei der man an seine Grenzen stösst, hinausgehende Problematik beschrieb. Es war eher so, als ob ich in einem kleinem Glaskasten eingeschlossen wäre, wo es mir nicht möglich war, mich zu meiner vollen Größe aufzurichten, geschweige denn mich nach oben oder auch nur zur Seite oder rückwärts zu bewegen. Jetzt, da ich dauerhaft in Deutschland lebe, habe ich deutlich mehr Spielraum. (2014, Seite 8)

Seit ich über die Gründe meines Umzuges nach Deutschland schrieb, hat sich die politische Situation in Großbritannien immer weiter nach rechts entwickelt. Insbesondere hat der Brexit eine massive Spaltung der Gesellschaft hervorgerufen. Als Bürgerin der Europäischen Union hatte ich von der Freizügigkeit innerhalb der EU profitiert, doch nun wird das Leben leider deutlich komplizierter. Wie Hendrick, der für den Rest seines Lebens in Haarlem blieb, werde ich niemals zurück nach Großbritannien ziehen. Es wäre finanziell unmöglich;

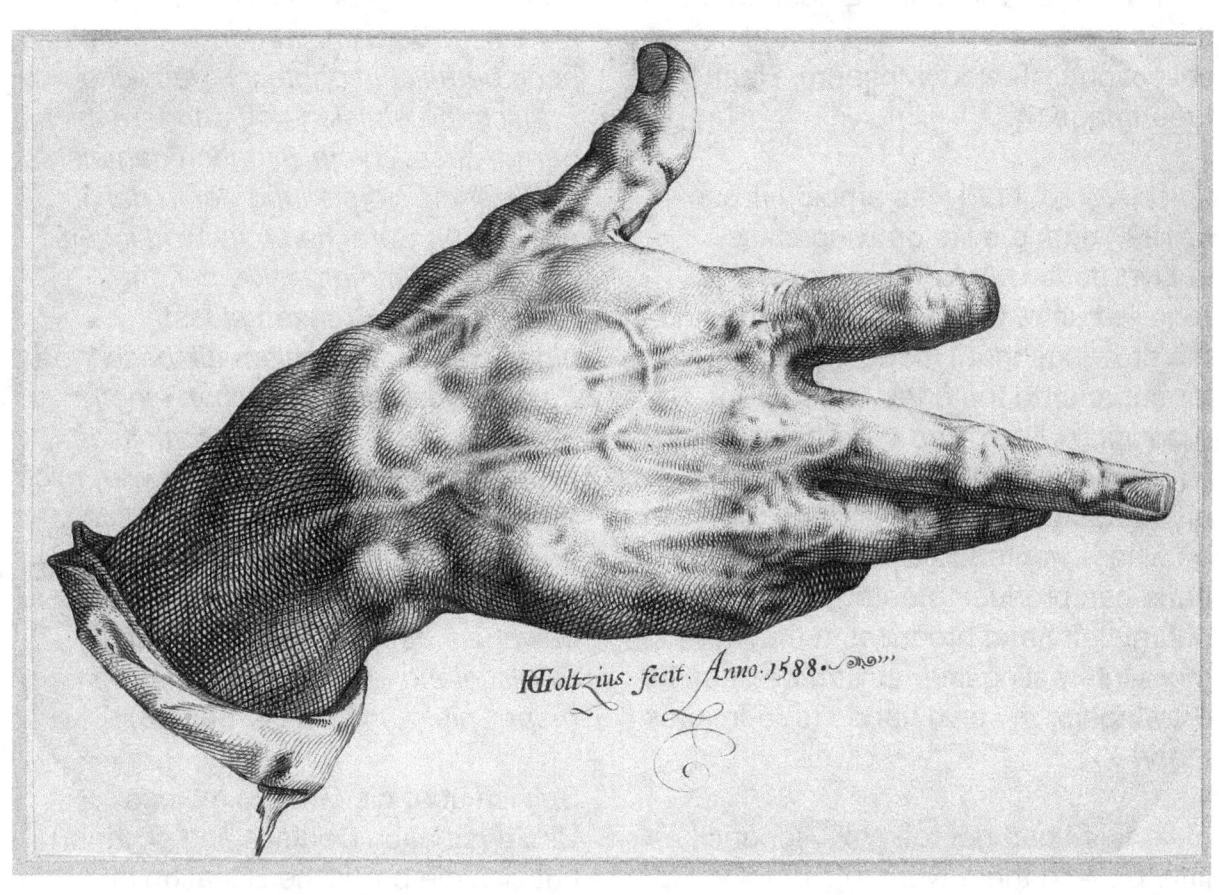

Image 5: Hendrick Goltzius, *Goltzius's Right Hand*, 1588, pen and brown ink on paper, 23 x 32.2 cm. Reproduced with kind permission from Teylers Museum, Haarlem

Darstellung 5: Hendrick Goltzius, *Goltzius' rechte Hand*, 1588, Füller und braune Tinte auf Papier, 23 x 32,2 cm. Reproduziert mit freundlicher Genehmigung des Teylers Museums, Haarlem

dramatically changed my view and the purpose of the project.

I had travelled to Haarlem to talk to someone who was no longer there – so I should have expected that there would be no response, but I was left feeling empty nonetheless. The drawings I made in Haarlem originate from this position of absence. Could I replace Hendrick with other people in Haarlem? Would other people be interested in talking about life drawing, human anatomy, class, politics, immigration and being ambidextrous?

I didn't speak to anybody about these topics, because I knew it would have been a fruitless endeavour. However, I realised that by drawing the people I saw there that day, I could create my own connection with Haarlem. In this way I could also – albeit indirectly – increase my connection with Hendrick in some small way.

The process of making the drawings started by selecting various traits of the individuals around me. I was interested in their shape, or the way that they moved, or something that they were wearing. I enjoyed watching the different people and imagining their lives for a moment. Of course, I did not draw every person that walked past that day, but of the people I drew I was aware of an exchange of energy, I saw their interactions with each other and with their environment, how they presented themselves to the world and what they were doing in that moment, for example smoking a cigarette or waiting for a bus, and I responded by making a line on the paper in front of me. These interactions may initially appear to be one-sided, and indeed my relationships with these

aber, was noch viel wichtiger ist, es wäre von einem persönlichen, kulturellen oder politischen Standpunkt aus undenkbar.

Außer, dass wir beide Künstler und Migranten sind, ist die auffälligste Gemeinsamkeit zwischen Hendrick und mir die Tatsache, dass wir beide beidhändig geschickt sind, also in der Lage sind, Kunst sowohl mit der rechten als auch mit der linken Hand zu schaffen. Als Hendrick noch klein war, verbrannte er seine rechte Hand bei einem Unfall. "Er war in ein Feuer geraten und die verbrannte rechte Hand verkrampfte sich so, dass er sie dauerhaft nicht öffnen konnte" (Mayor, 1971, Seite 419). In Folge dieser Beeinträchtigung konnte er nur sein Werkzeug in der rechten Hand halten, wobei er die Muskeln seines Oberarms und seiner Schulter verwenden musste, um es zu bewegen und mit ihm zu arbeiten. In einer Biografie Hendricks vertritt Karel van Mander die Ansicht, dass Hendrick zum Kupferstechen die rechte und zum Zeichnen die linke Hand verwendete (1604, Seite 282). Ein Beleg dafür ist die Zeichnung von Hendricks rechter Hand in der Sammlung des Teylers Museum in Haarlem (Darstellung 5).

Ich fand 1997 bei einem Zeichenkurs in Liverpool in Großbritannien heraus, dass ich mit beiden Händen Kunst schaffen kann. Wir sollten bei einer Zeichenübung unsere "andere" Hand einsetzen und die Zeichnungen, die ich an jenem Tag anfertigte, waren weit besser als die, die ich zuvor mit meiner "starken" Hand angefertigt hatte. Seit jenem Tag setze ich beim Zeichnen beide Hände abwechselnd

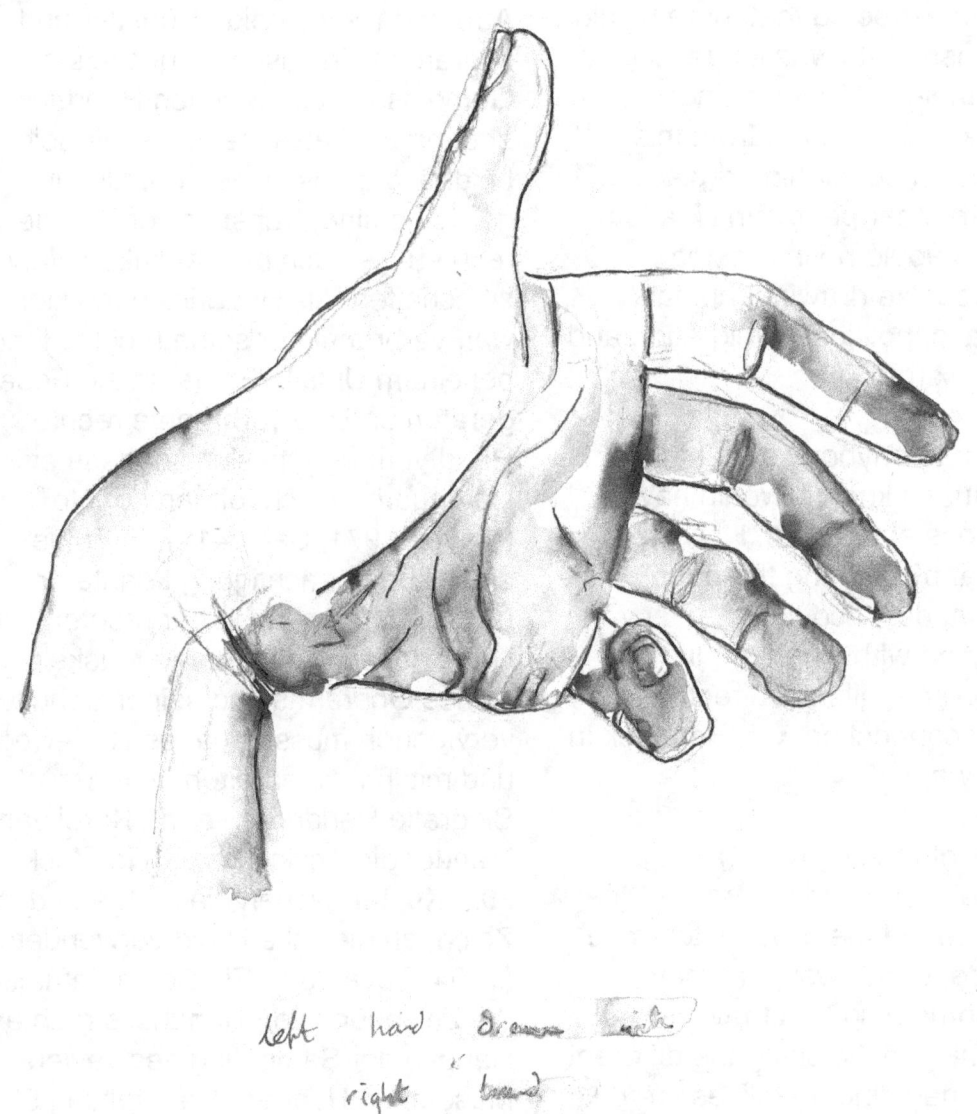

left hand *drawn* *with*

right *hand*

03/11/2018

Image 6: *Conversations on Falling: left hand drawn with right hand*, 2018, ink and pencil on paper, 42 x 28.8 cm

Darstellung 6: *Konversationen über das Fallen: linke Hand, mit der rechten Hand gezeichnet*, 2018, Tinte und Bleistift auf Papier, 42 x 28,8 cm

people only lasted mere seconds, but an exchange did take place and it was this exchange that became my surrogate for a conversation.

A significant amount of information is absent in the drawings. But as in any good conversation, much can be said without words (or lines in this case). Most often, there is only a suggestion of a figure, a simple line forms each person. With this lack of formal information, you, the viewer, are required to do some work – to fill the gaps and make sense of the drawing. There is also an absence of information about the individuals in the drawings, who are these people, where are they going, what are they thinking? But even if I had spoken to the people in the drawings, a complete picture is unachievable because even after years of building relationships full knowledge of another person is impossible.

I captured the people who walked through my frame of reference that day as just a mark on the paper, and then they were gone again. They were unaware of this exchange, but I responded to the information they gave me in that moment. When I draw in public places, both in Haarlem and anywhere else, I have an unwritten contract with my subjects that I do not interfere in their movements. I do not want to make them feel uncomfortable, so I never stare intently at them and I only draw them while I can see them. I have at most a few seconds to draw someone, often as they briskly walk past, and then they are gone. This project, however, has taken significantly longer than a few seconds to complete. I have been working on this publication for more than two years. The

ein, abhängig davon, welches Ziel ich bei der Erstellung des Werks verfolge. Während ich mit meiner rechten Hand genauer arbeiten kann, schafft meine linke Hand eine interessantere Linienführung, wie in den Zeichnungen meiner Hände zu sehen ist (Darstellungen 6 und 7).

Ich hatte das Gefühl, Hendrick ein wenig kennengelernt zu haben und es gab viele Dinge, über die ich mit ihm sprechen wollte - so ist es verständlich, dass ich ihn "treffen" wollte. Ende 2018 plante ich, nach Haarlem zu fahren, um die Möglichkeit zu haben, dort durch die Straßen zu gehen, wo er gelebt und gewirkt hatte. Mit dem Zug fuhr ich von meinem Haus in Niederbrechen in Deutschland nach Amsterdam und von dort aus nach Haarlem, aber es wurde mir sehr schnell klar, dass ich Hendrick nirgends finden konnte... Ich bin nicht sicher, was genau meine Erwartungen gewesen waren, als ich nach Haarlem fuhr, aber ich fühlte Hendricks Abwesenheit sehr stark. Dieses Gefühl wirkte sich massiv auf meine Sichtweise und die Ausrichtung des Projekts aus.

Ich war nach Haarlem gekommen, um mit jemandem zu sprechen, der nicht mehr dort war - also hätte ich diese Reaktion voraussehen können; nichtsdestotrotz fühlte ich eine innere Leere. Hendricks Abwesenheit inspirierte die Zeichnungen, die ich in Haarlem anfertigte. Würde ich Hendrick durch andere Menschen in Haarlem ersetzen können? Würden andere Menschen überhaupt Interesse daran haben, über Zeichnen, menschliche Anatomie, Gesellschaftsschichten, Politik, Immigration und das Schaffen von Kunst mit beiden Händen zu

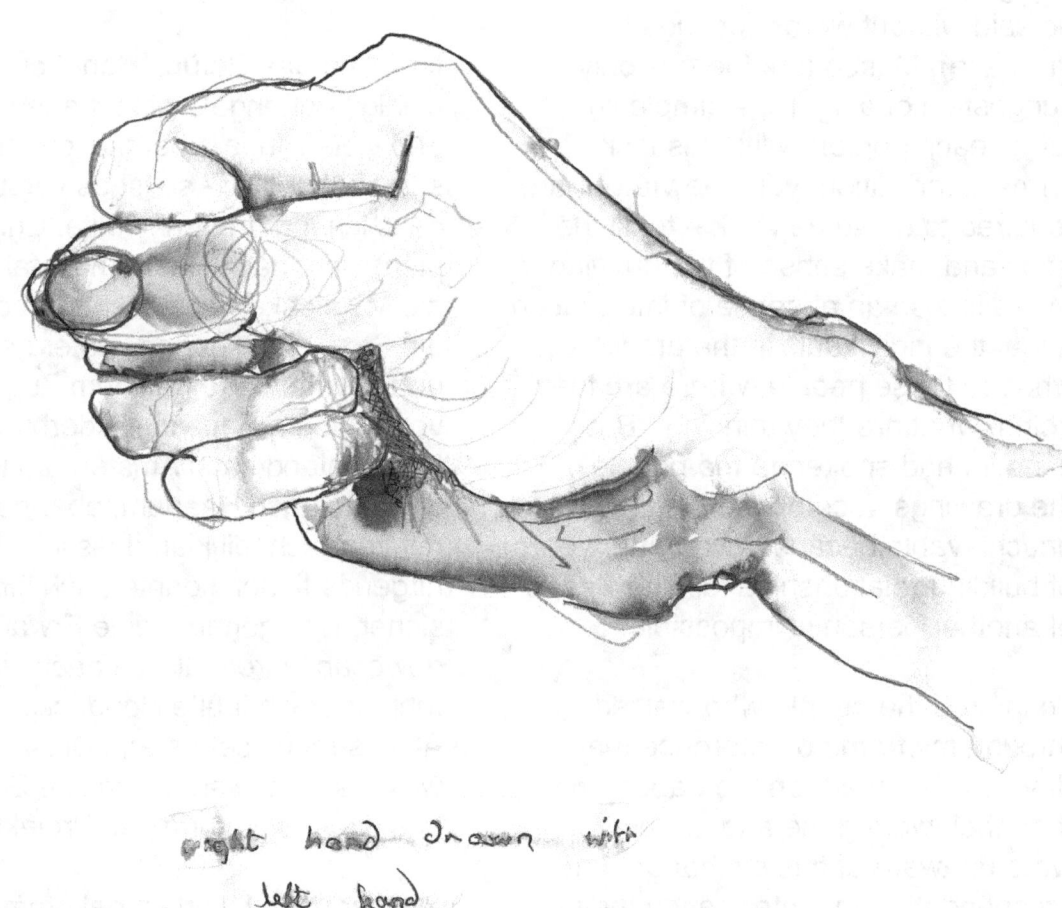

right hand drawn with
left hand

044/11/2018

Image 7: *Conversations on Falling: right hand drawn with left hand*, 2018, ink and pencil on paper, 42 x 28.8 cm

Darstellung 7: *Konversationen über das Fallen: rechte Hand, mit der linken Hand gezeichnet*, 2018, Tinte und Bleistift auf Papier, 42 x 28,8 cm

process of making this book has been rewarding though, not only because I have had the opportunity to think – both through making drawings and thinking about them afterwards – but also that my practice has developed as a result of the process. By looking at the drawings on the following pages it is unlikely that you will get to know Hendrick any better, because I certainly wasn't able to, but you will see something of the people that were in Haarlem on 26th December 2018 going about their ordinary business and the brief exchange that took place when I drew them.

References:
Mayor, A. Hyatt (1971) *Prints & People: a social history of printed pictures*, Princeton, New Jersey: Princeton University Press.

Pelling, Kate (2014) *[Video] Klappe*, Frankfurt am Main/London: Fifth Floor Publications.

Van Mander, Karel (1604) *Het schilder-boeck* (facsimile of the first edition created in 1969), Utrecht: Davaco Publishers. Available at: http://www.dbnl.org/tekst/mand001schi01_01/colofon.htm [Accessed 11 February 2020].

sprechen?

Ich sprach mit niemandem über diese Themen, da ich wusste, dass dies ein hoffnungsloses Unterfangen gewesen wäre. Dennoch erkannte ich, dass ich durch das Zeichnen der Menschen, die ich an jenem Tag dort sah, meine eigene Verbindung zu Haarlem schaffen konnte. So konnte ich auch, und sei es auch indirekt, meine Verbindung zu Hendrick ein wenig intensivieren.

Der Prozess des Zeichnens begann mit der Auswahl verschiedener Charakterzüge der Menschen um mich herum. Ich interessierte mich für ihre Umrisse, die Art, wie sie sich bewegten oder dafür, welche Kleidung sie trugen. Es machte mir Freude, verschiedene Menschen zu sehen und mir einen Moment lang vorzustellen, wie sie lebten. Natürlich zeichnete ich nicht alle Menschen, die mir an jenem Tag begegneten. Doch war ich mir im Hinblick auf die von mir gezeichneten Menschen bewusst, dass wir Energie austauschten; ich sah, wie sie miteinander und mit ihrer Umwelt interagierten, wie sie sich ihrer Umwelt präsentierten und was sie in jenem Moment taten, wie zum Beispiel eine Zigarette zu rauchen oder auf einen Bus zu warten, und ich reagierte darauf, indem ich auf dem Papier vor mir zu zeichnen begann. Auf den ersten Blick mögen diese Interaktionen einseitig erscheinen; und in der Tat, meine Verbindung zu diesen Menschen dauerte nur einige Sekunden, doch fand ein Austausch statt, der für mich zum Ersatz für eine Konversation wurde.

Eine große Menge Informationen ist aus den Zeichnungen nicht ersichtlich. Aber wie in jeder guten Konversation kann

vieles ohne Worte (oder in diesem
Fall gezeichnete Linien) ausgedrückt
werden. Meist ist nur die Andeutung
einer Figur zu sehen, eine einfache
Linie stellt die Person dar. Diese
Abwesenheit der formalen Information
ist eine Einladung an den Betrachter,
selbst etwas zu leisten - die Lücken
zu füllen und den Sinn der Zeichnung
zu erschließen. Auch liegen keine
Informationen über die Menschen auf
den Zeichnungen vor. Wer sind diese
Menschen? Wohin gehen sie? Was
denken sie? Doch selbst wenn ich mit
den Menschen auf den Zeichnungen
gesprochen hätte, könnte kein
Gesamtbild erreicht werden, denn auch
nach vielen Jahren des gegenseitigen
Kennens ist es unmöglich, alles über
einen anderen Menschen zu wissen.

Ich fing die Menschen, die an jenem
Tag durch meinen Bezugsrahmen
liefen, einfach als Linien auf dem
Papier ein; dann waren sie wieder
verschwunden. Sie waren sich dieses
Austausches nicht bewusst, aber ich
reagierte auf die Informationen, die sie
mir in jenem Moment zur Verfügung
stellten. Wenn ich in der Öffentlichkeit
zeichne, sei es in Haarlem oder an
irgendeinem anderen Ort, so habe ich
stets die ungeschriebene Übereinkunft
mit den Menschen, die ich zeichne,
das, was sie gerade tun nicht zu
stören. Ich möchte nicht, dass sie
sich unwohl fühlen, also starre ich
sie niemals an und zeichne sie nur
so lange, wie ich sie sehen kann. Mir
bleiben höchstens einige Sekunden, um
einen Menschen zu zeichnen, der eilig
vorbeiläuft; dann ist er verschwunden.
Doch dauerte diese Projekt deutlich
länger als einige Sekunden. Ich habe
an ihm mehr als zwei Jahre lang

gearbeitet. Es war dennoch eine sehr lohnende Erfahrung, dieses Buch zu schaffen, nicht nur, weil es mir die Gelegenheit gab, viel nachzudenken, sowohl durch das Zeichnen als auch durch das Reflektieren der gefertigten Zeichnungen, sondern auch durch einen enormen Gewinn an neuen Erfahrungen und Zeichenpraxis. Durch den Blick auf die Zeichnungen auf den folgenden Seiten wird der Betrachter Hendrick höchstwahrscheinlich nicht besser kennenlernen können, da dies auch mir nicht gelang, doch wird er die Menschen sehen, die am 26. Dezember 2018 in Haarlem ihren ganz normalen Tätigkeiten nachgingen und etwas über den kurzen Austausch erfahren, der stattfand, als ich sie zeichnete.

Quellenangaben:
Mayor, A. Hyatt (1971) *Prints & People: a social history of printed pictures*, Princeton, New Jersey: Princeton University Press

Pelling, Kate (2014) *[Video] Klappe*, Frankfurt am Main/London: Fifth Floor Publications

Van Mander, Karel (1604) *Het schilder-boeck* (Faksimile der ersten Ausgabe, 1969), Utrecht: Davaco Publishers. Erhältlich bei: http://www.dbnl.org/tekst/ mand001schi01_01/colofon.htm [11. Februar 2020].

Haarlem

26th December 2018 / 26. Dezember 2018

Two men walking by with pizza boxes and shopping bags, Haarlem, 2018, ink on paper, 21 x 29.7 cm

Zwei Männer laufen mit Pizzaschachteln und Einkaufstüten vorbei, Haarlem, 2018, Tinte auf Papier, 21 x 29,7 cm

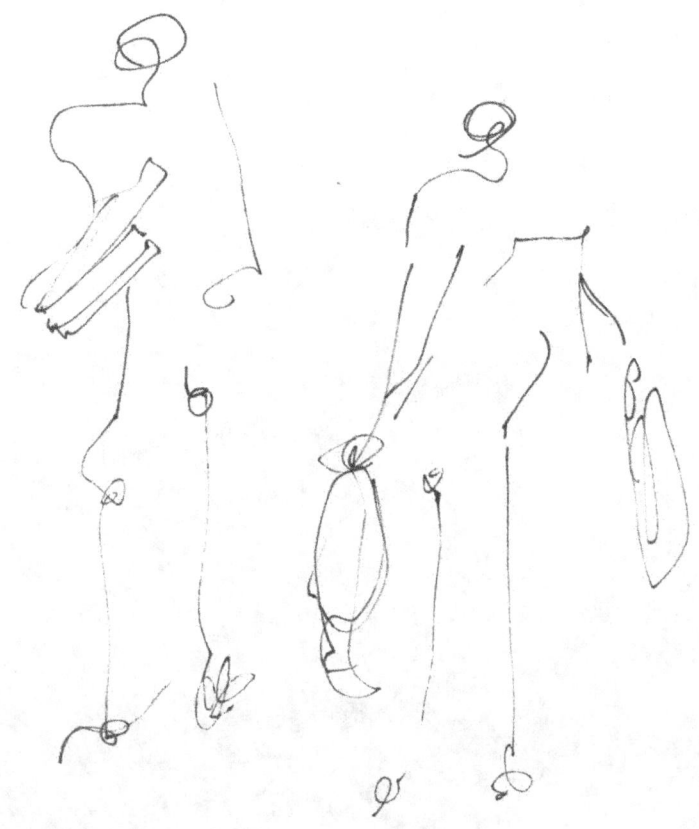

2 men walking by with pizza boxes
and shopping bags. Haarlem 26/12/2018

Man waiting for a bus, Haarlem, 2018, ink on paper, 21 x 29.7 cm

Mann wartet auf einen Bus, Haarlem, 2018, Tinte auf Papier, 21 x 29,7 cm

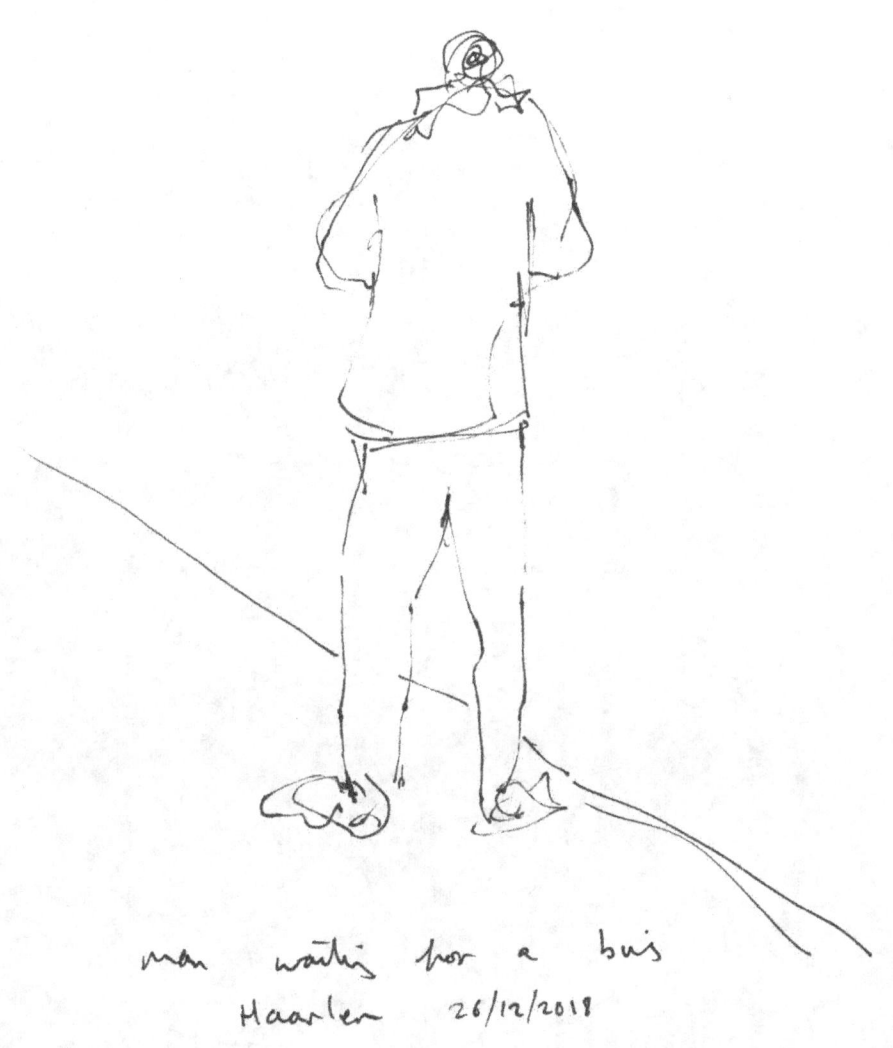

man waiting for a bus
Haarlem 26/12/2018

Woman with large bag waiting for a bus,
Haarlem, 2018, ink on paper, 21 x 29.7 cm

Frau mit großer Tasche wartet auf einen Bus,
Haarlem, 2018, Tinte auf Papier, 21 x 29,7 cm

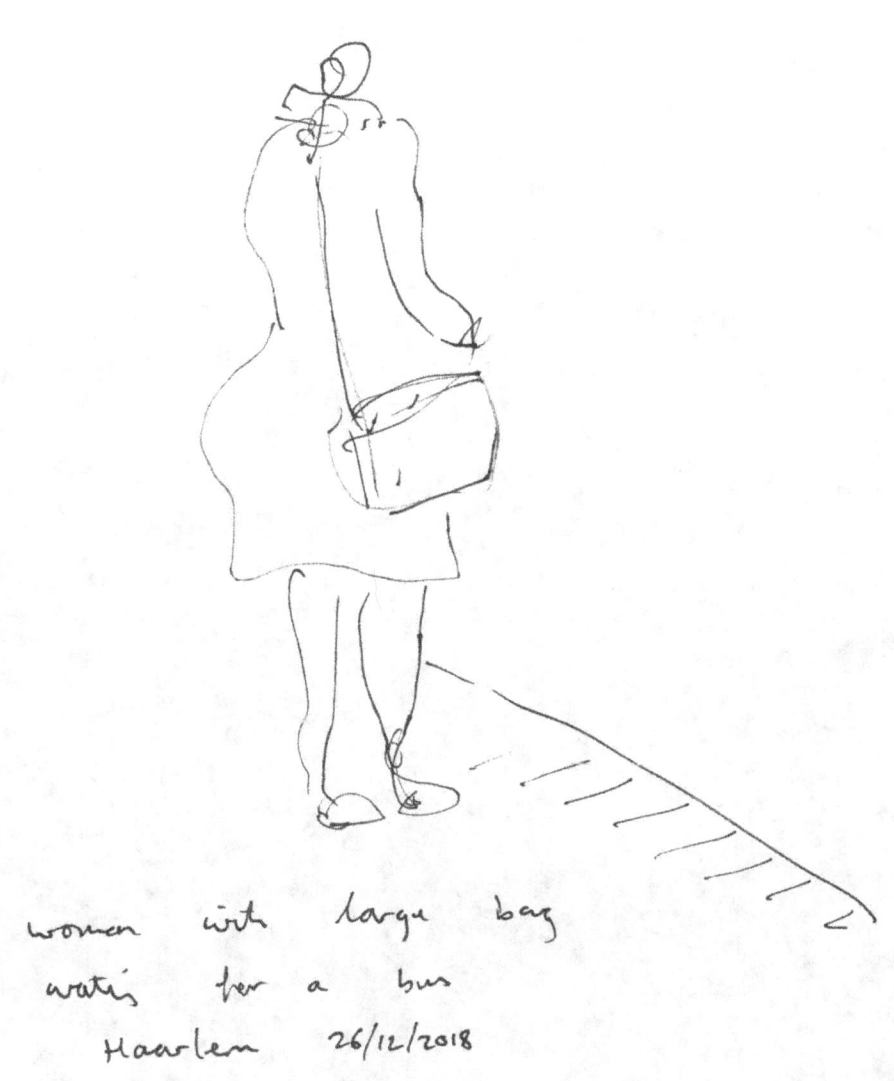

woman with large bag
waits for a bus
Haarlem 26/12/2018

Man with headphones walking along the canal,
Haarlem, 2018, ink on paper, 21 x 29.7 cm

*Mann mit Kopfhörern, die entlang des Kanals
gehen*, Haarlem, 2018, Tinte auf Papier,
21 x 29,7 cm

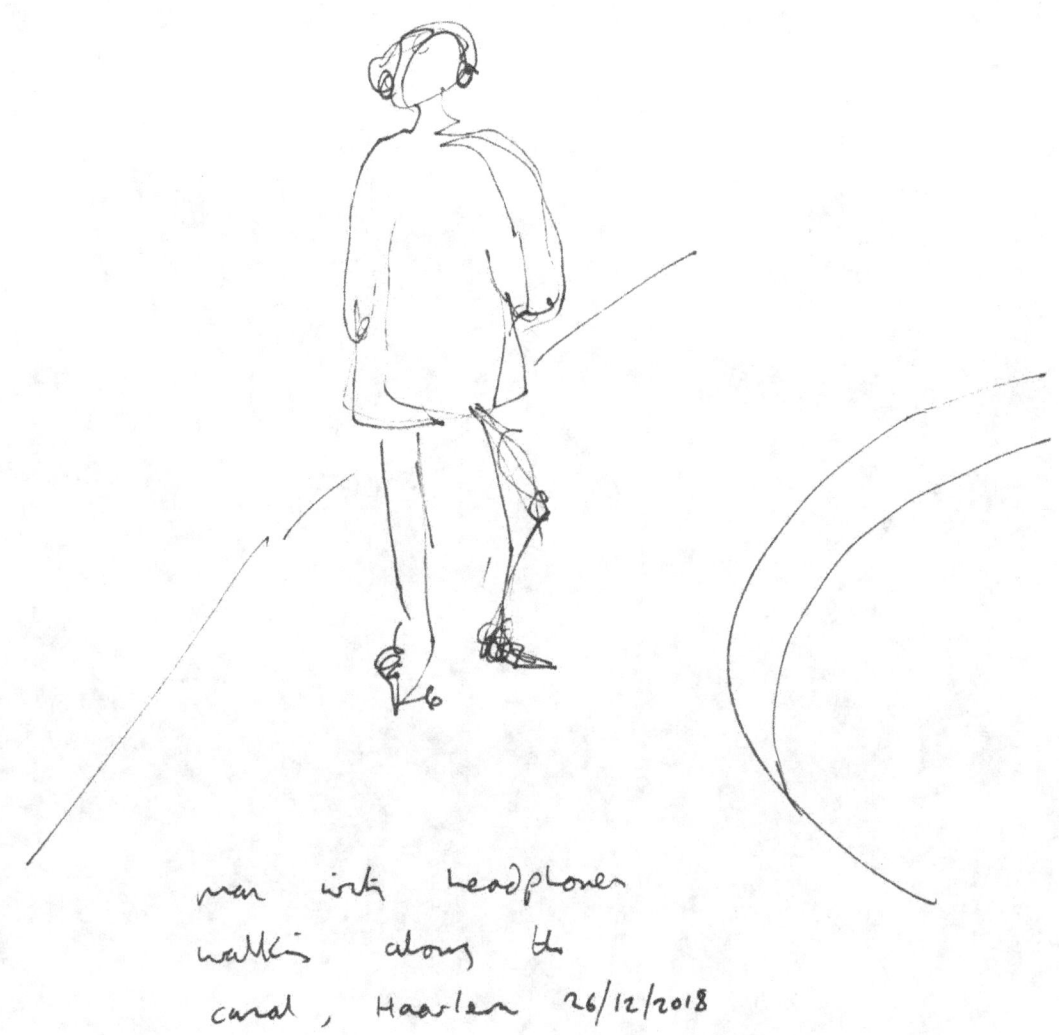

man with headphones
walking along the
canal, Haarlem 26/12/2018

Woman on a bike, Haarlem, 2018, ink on paper,
21 x 29.7 cm

Frau auf einem Fahrrad, Haarlem, 2018, Tinte auf
Papier, 21 x 29,7 cm

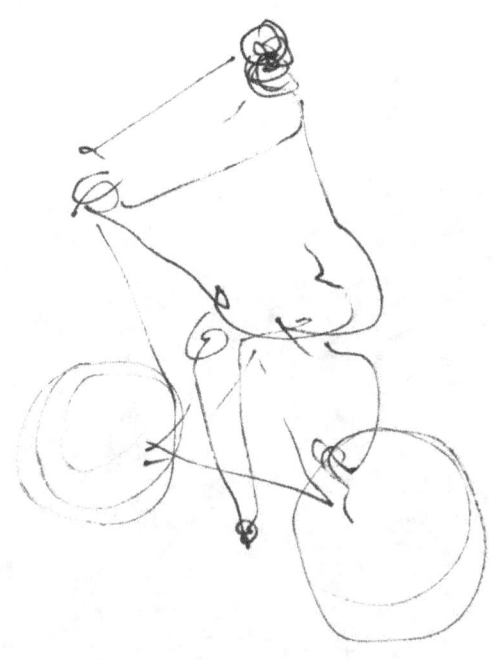

woman on a bike
Haarlen   26/12/2018

Two women walking past, Haarlem, 2018, ink on paper, 21 x 29.7 cm

Zwei Frauen laufen vorbei, Haarlem, 2018, Tinte auf Papier, 21 x 29,7 cm

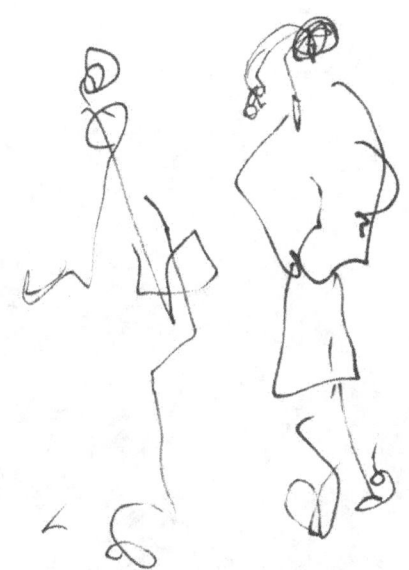

Two women walking past
Haarlem 26/12/2018

Man walking in Haarlem, 2018, ink on paper,
21 x 29.7 cm

Laufender Mann in Haarlem, 2018, Tinte auf
Papier, 21 x 29,7 cm

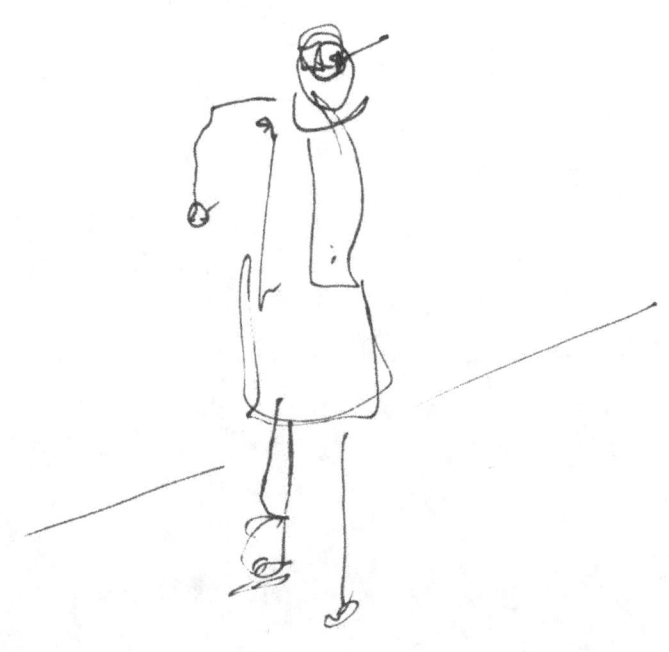

man walking in Haarlem
26/12/2018

Two tourists, Haarlem, 2018, ink on paper,
21 x 29.7 cm

Zwei Touristen, Haarlem, 2018, Tinte auf Papier,
21 x 29,7 cm

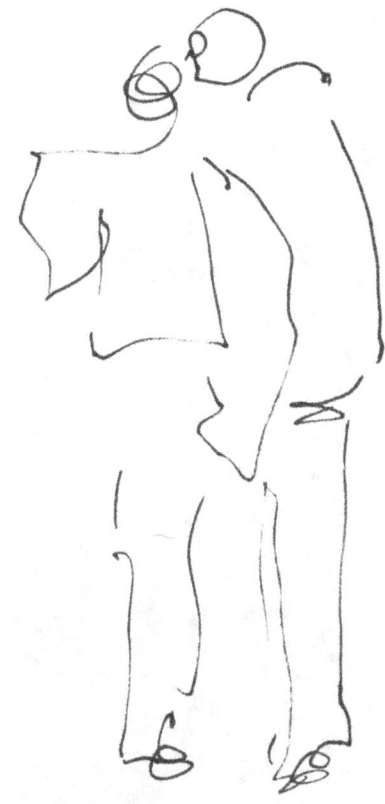

two tourists   Haarlem 26/12/2018

Man on the phone, Haarlem, 2018, ink on paper,
21 x 29.7 cm

Mann telefoniert, Haarlem, 2018, Tinte auf Papier,
21 x 29,7 cm

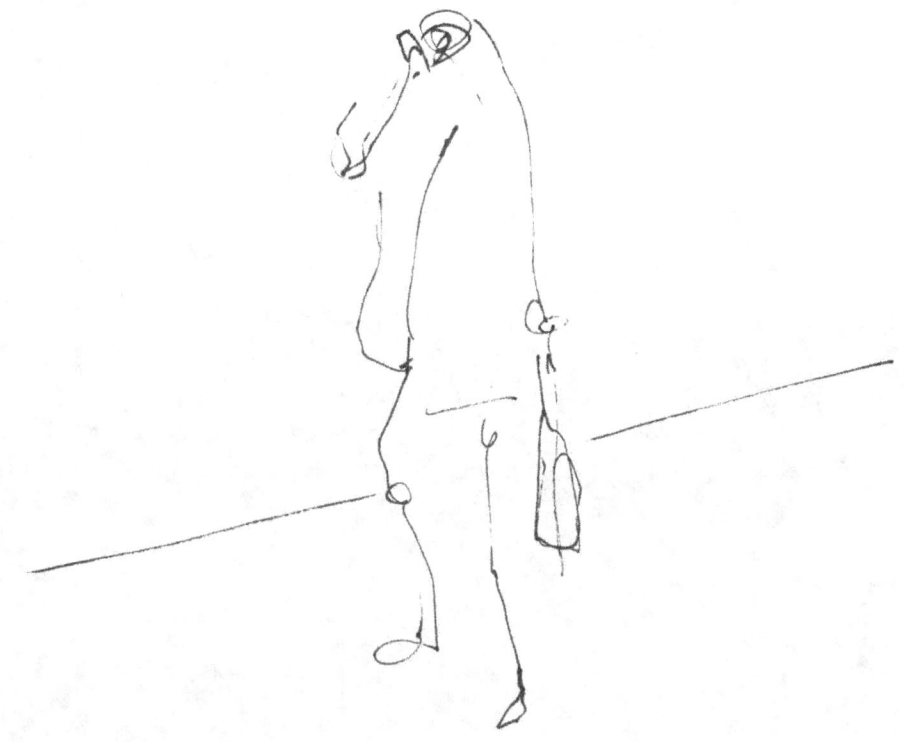

man on the phone
Haarlem 26/12/2018

Man walking his dog, Haarlem, 2018, ink on paper, 21 x 29.7 cm

Mann führt seinen Hund spazieren, Haarlem, 2018, Tinte auf Papier, 21 x 29,7 cm

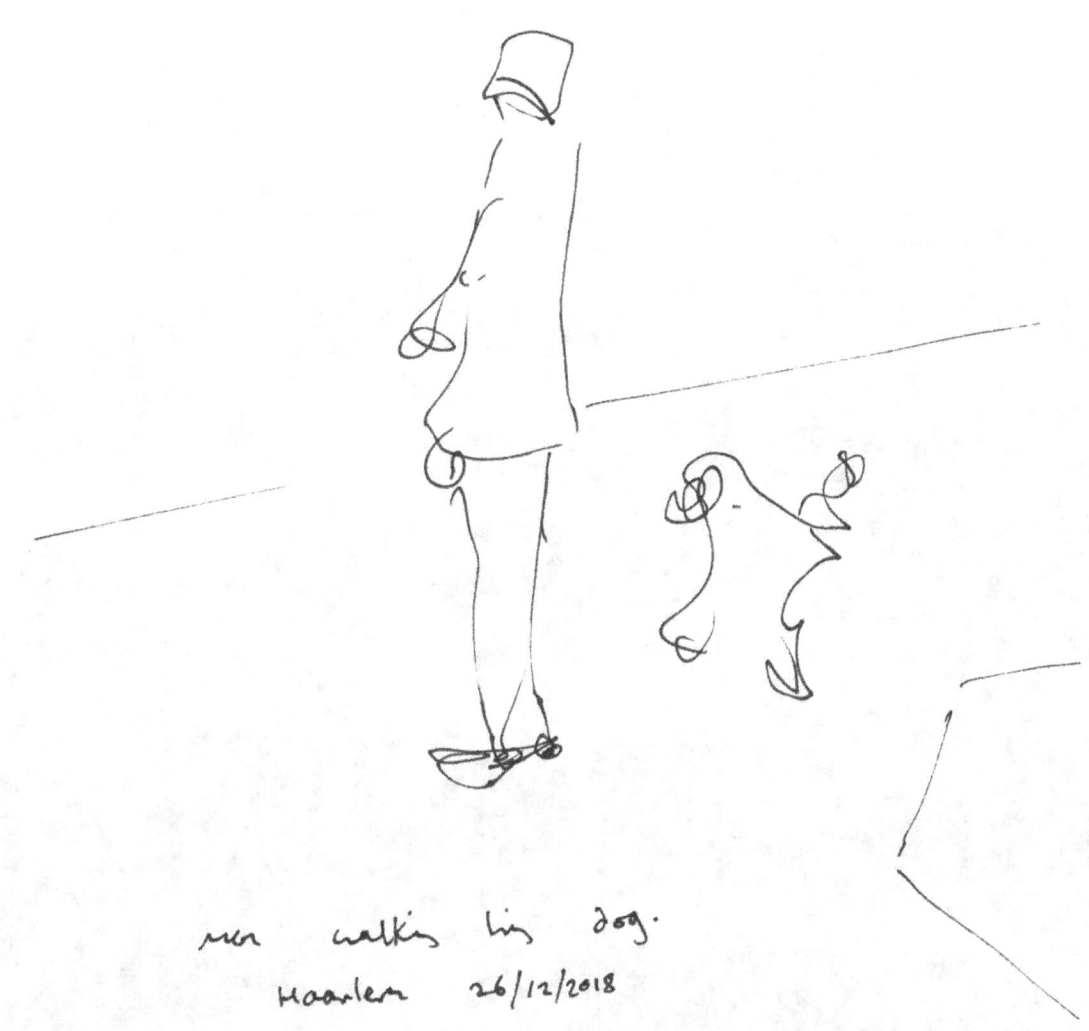

man walking his dog.
Haarlem 26/12/2018

Group of people walking past, Haarlem, 2018, ink on paper, 21 x 29.7 cm

Gruppe von Menschen läuft vorbei, Haarlem, 2018, Tinte auf Papier, 21 x 29,7 cm

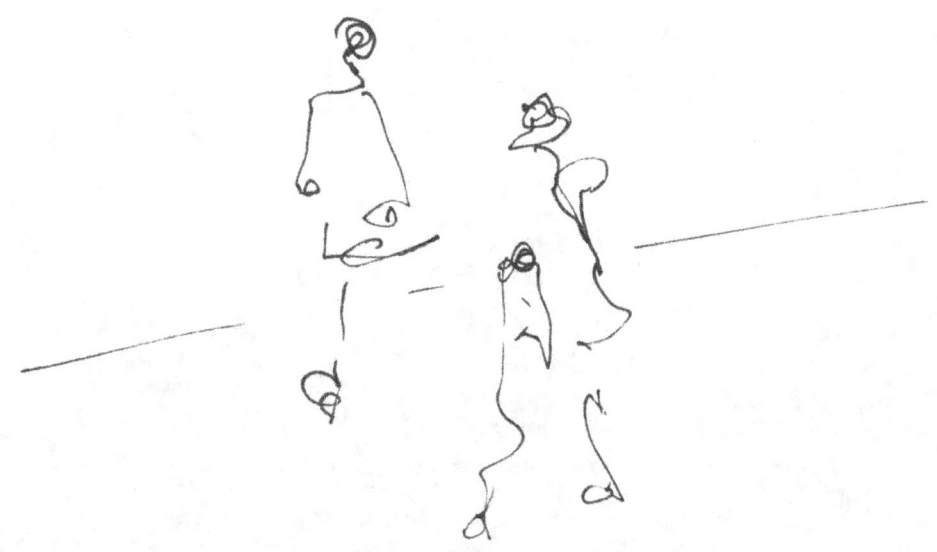

group of three people
walking past
Haarlem 26/12/2018

Man with a large bag opening an ornate door,
Haarlem, 2018, ink on paper, 21 x 29.7 cm

Mann mit einer großen Tasche öffnet eine
verzierte Tür, Haarlem, 2018, Tinte auf Papier,
21 x 29,7 cm

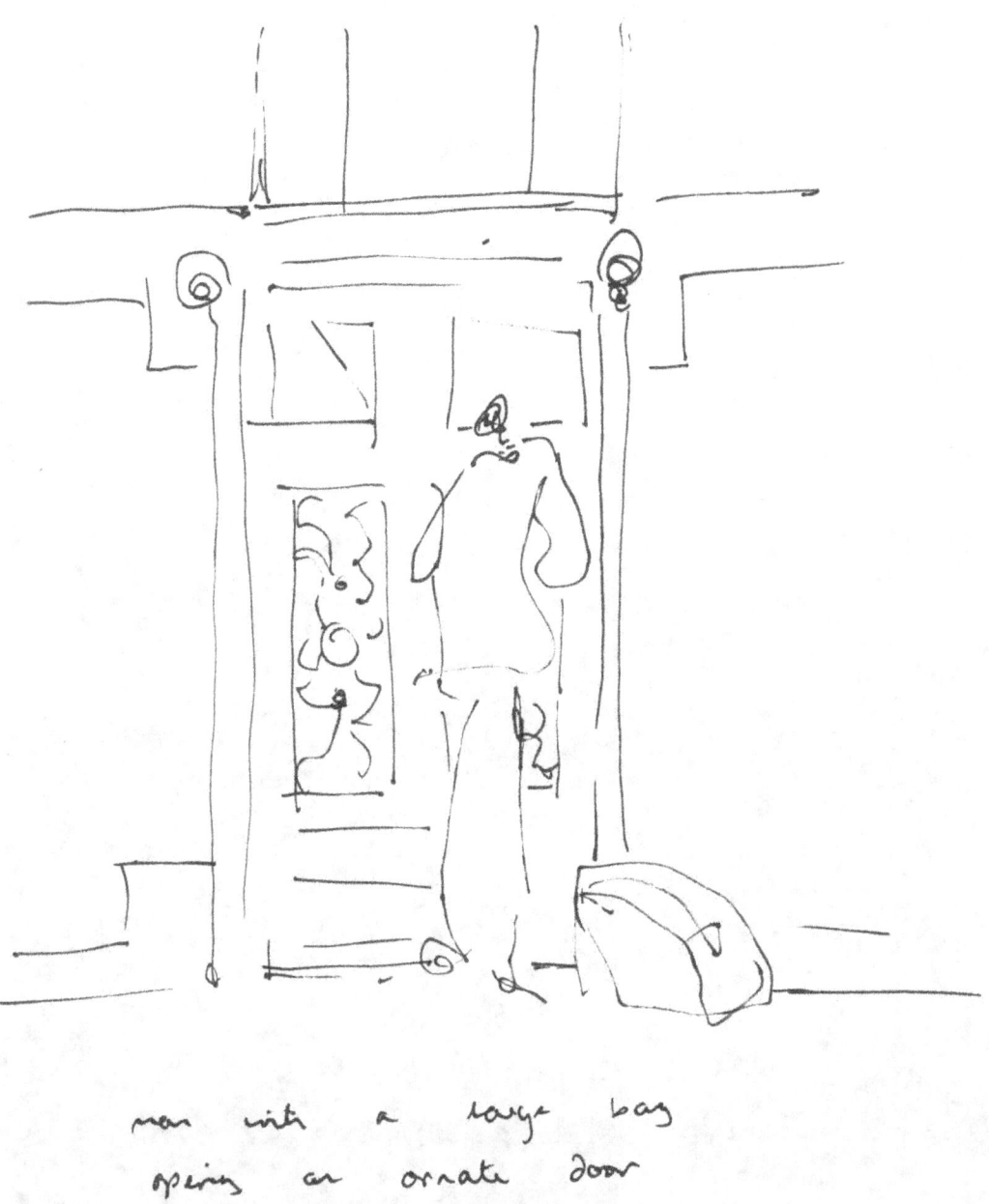

man with a large bag
opening an ornate door
Haarlem   26/12/2018

Woman with a trolley, Haarlem, 2018, ink on paper, 21 x 29.7 cm

Frau mit Einkaufstrolley, Haarlem, 2018, Tinte auf Papier, 21 x 29,7 cm

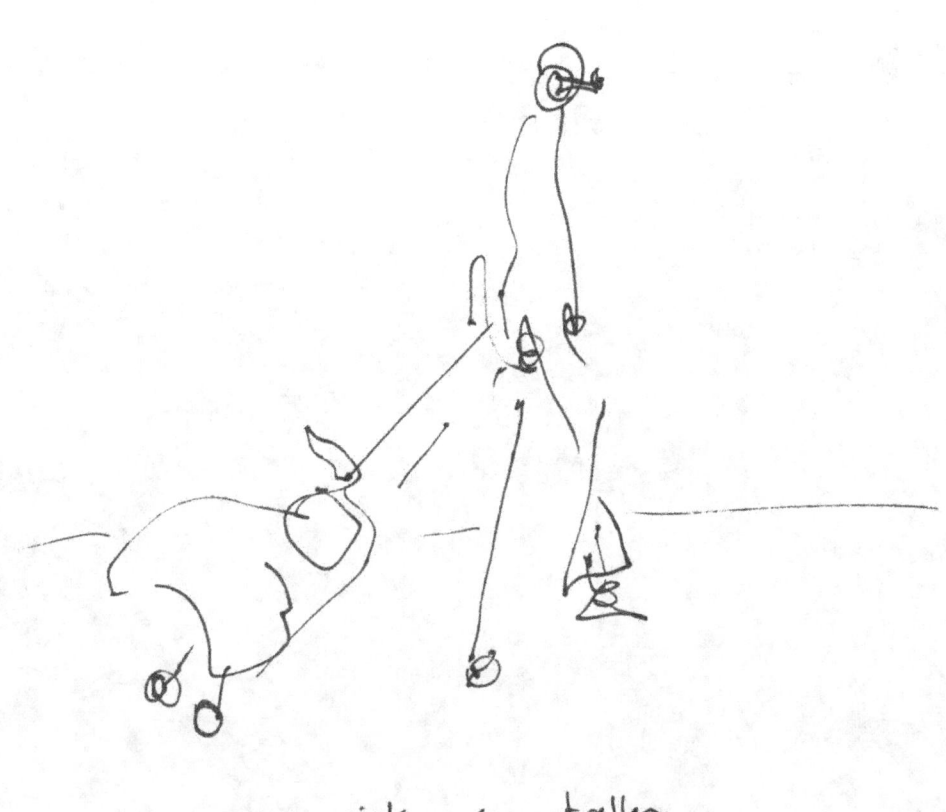

woman with a trolley
Haarlem 26/12/2018

Woman walking past, Haarlem, 2018, ink on
paper, 21 x 29.7 cm

Frau läuft vorbei, Haarlem, 2018, Tinte auf Papier,
21 x 29,7 cm

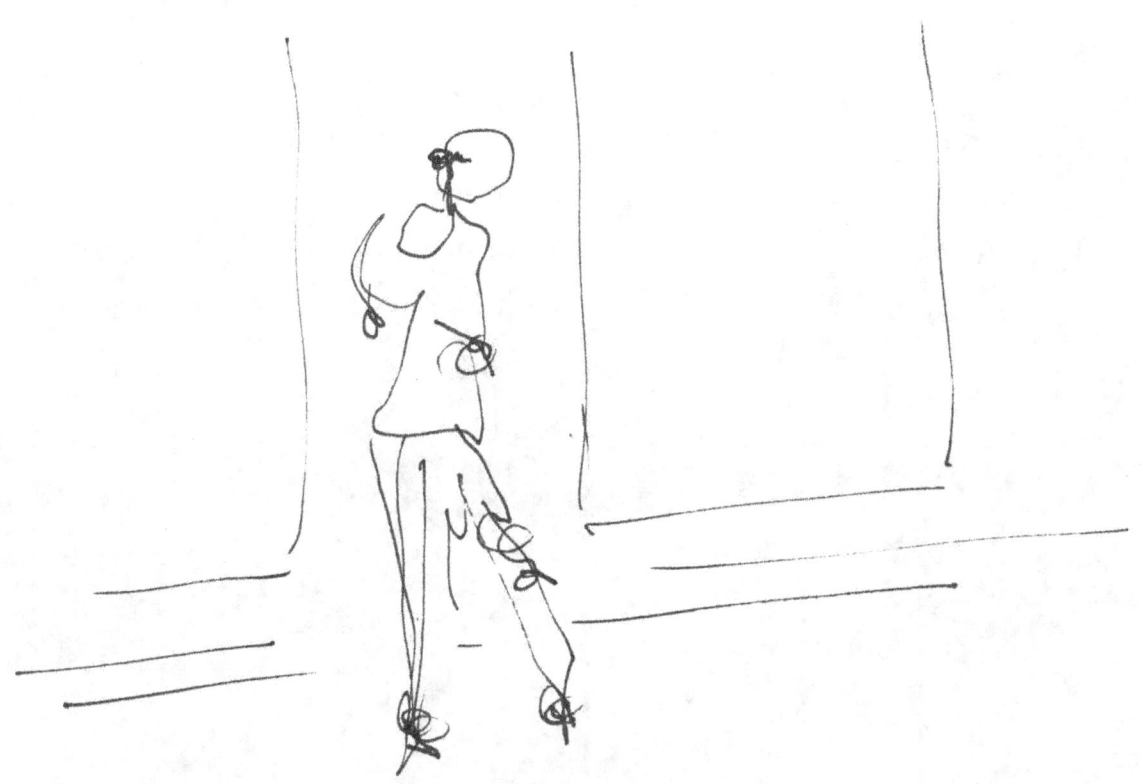

woman walks past
Haarlem 26/12/2018

Man on a bike, Haarlem, 2018, ink on paper, 21 x 29.7 cm

Mann auf dem Fahrrad, Haarlem, 2018, Tinte auf Papier, 21 x 29,7 cm

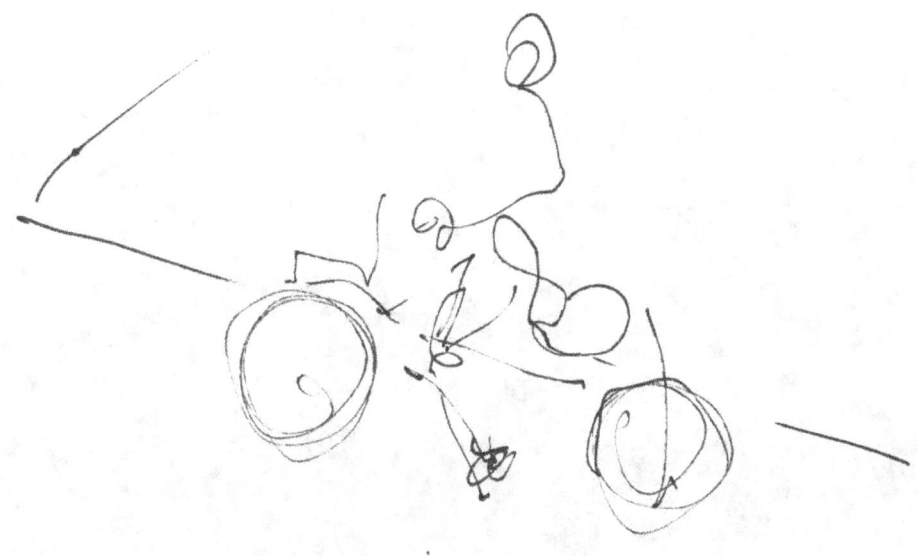

man on a bike
Haarlem 26/12/2018

Short man, Haarlem, 2018, ink on paper,
21 x 29.7 cm

Kleiner Mann, Haarlem, 2018, Tinte auf Papier,
21 x 29,7 cm

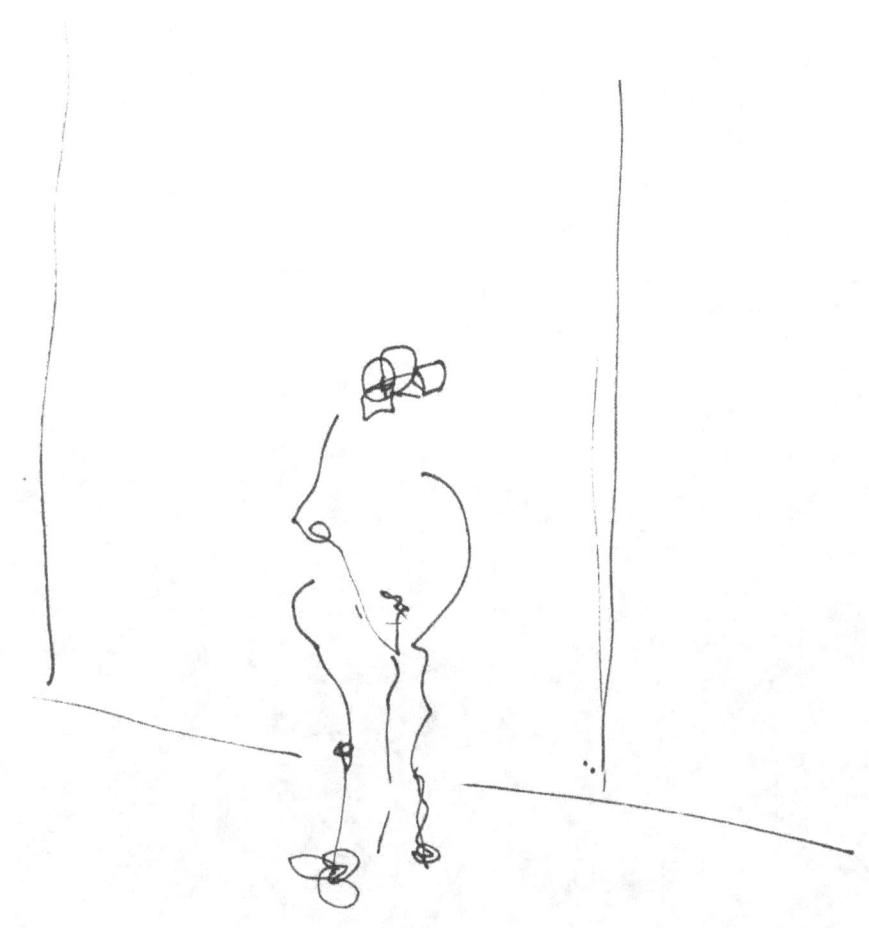

Short man Haarlem
26/12/2018

Man walking past, Haarlem, 2018, ink on paper,
21 x 29.7 cm

Mann läuft vorbei, Haarlem, 2018, Tinte auf Papier,
21 x 29,7 cm

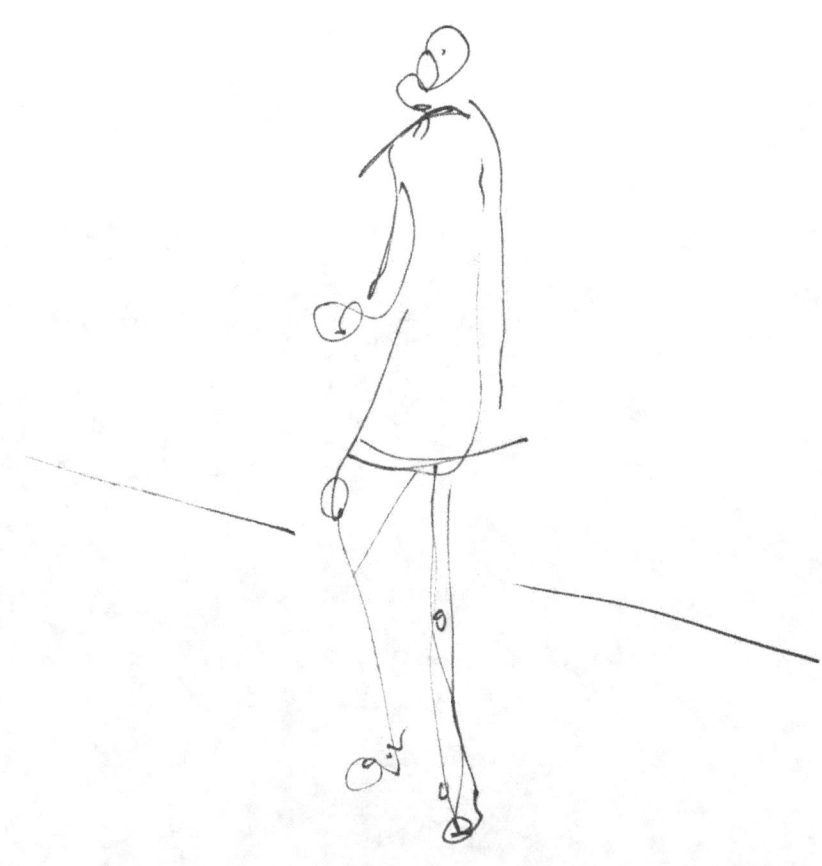

man walking past
Haarlem 26/12/2018

Woman in black with large bag, Haarlem, 2018,
ink on paper, 21 x 29.7 cm

Schwarz gekleidete Frau mit großer Tasche,
Haarlem, 2018, Tinte auf Papier, 21 x 29,7 cm

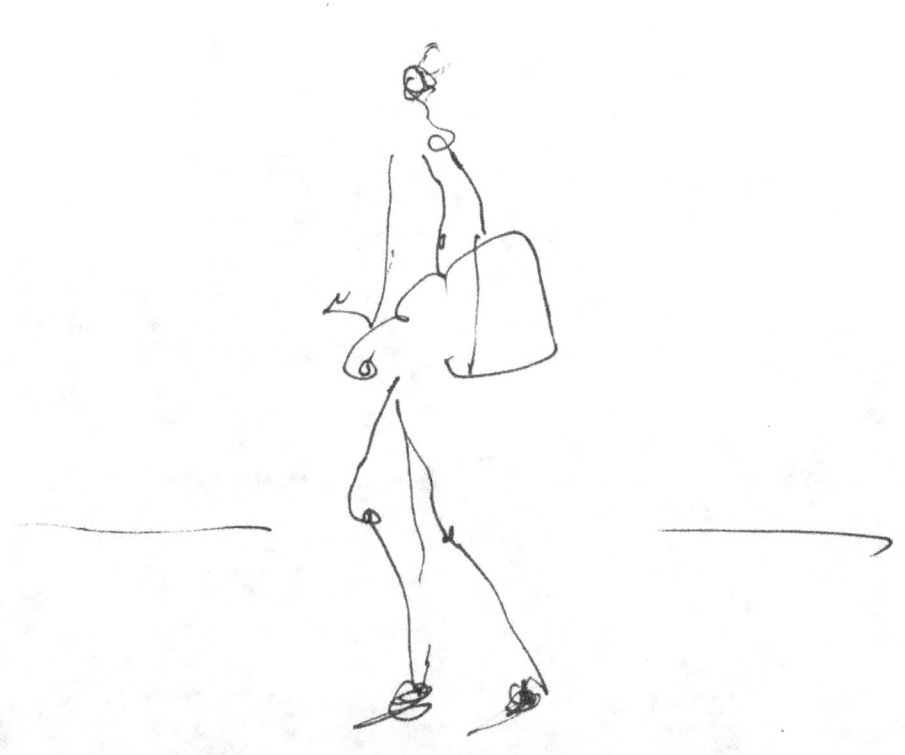

woman in black with
large bag. Haarlem.
26/12/2018.

Man and woman with baby in pram, Haarlem, 2018, ink on paper, 21 x 29.7 cm

Mann und Frau mit einem Baby im Kinderwagen, Haarlem, 2018, Tinte auf Papier, 21 x 29,7 cm

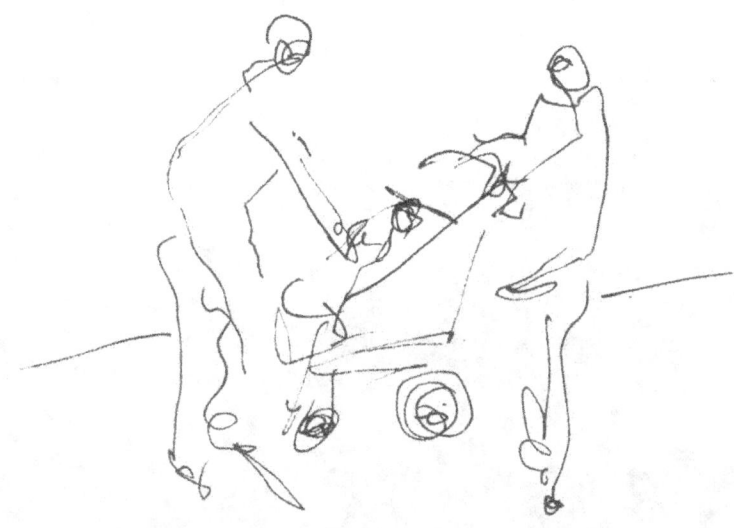

man and woman with
baby in pram
Haarlem   26/12/2018

Elderly couple, Haarlem, 2018, ink on paper,
21 x 29.7 cm

Älteres Paar, Haarlem, 2018, Tinte auf Papier,
21 x 29,7 cm

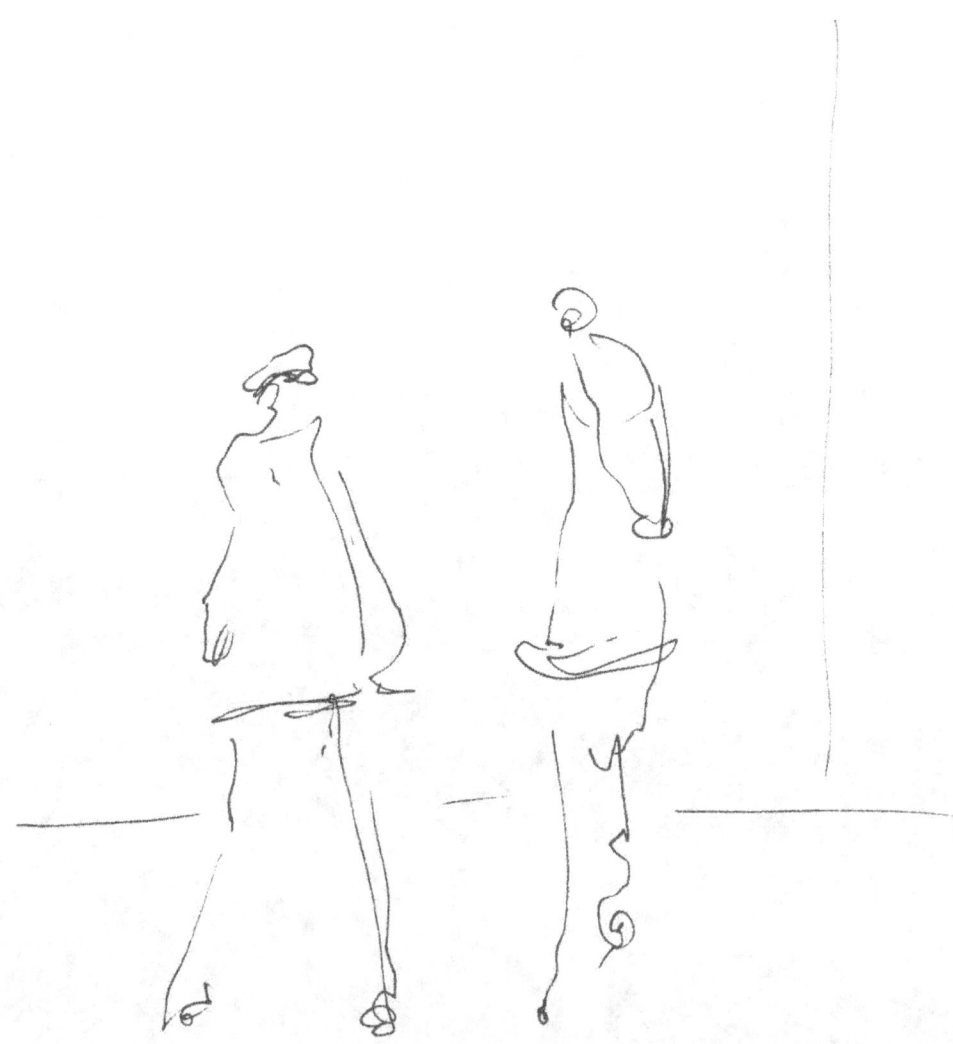

elderly couple Haarlem 26/12/2018

Fat guy in yellow jacket, Haarlem, 2018, ink on paper, 21 x 29.7 cm

Dicker Typ in gelber Jacke, Haarlem, 2018, Tinte auf Papier, 21 x 29,7 cm

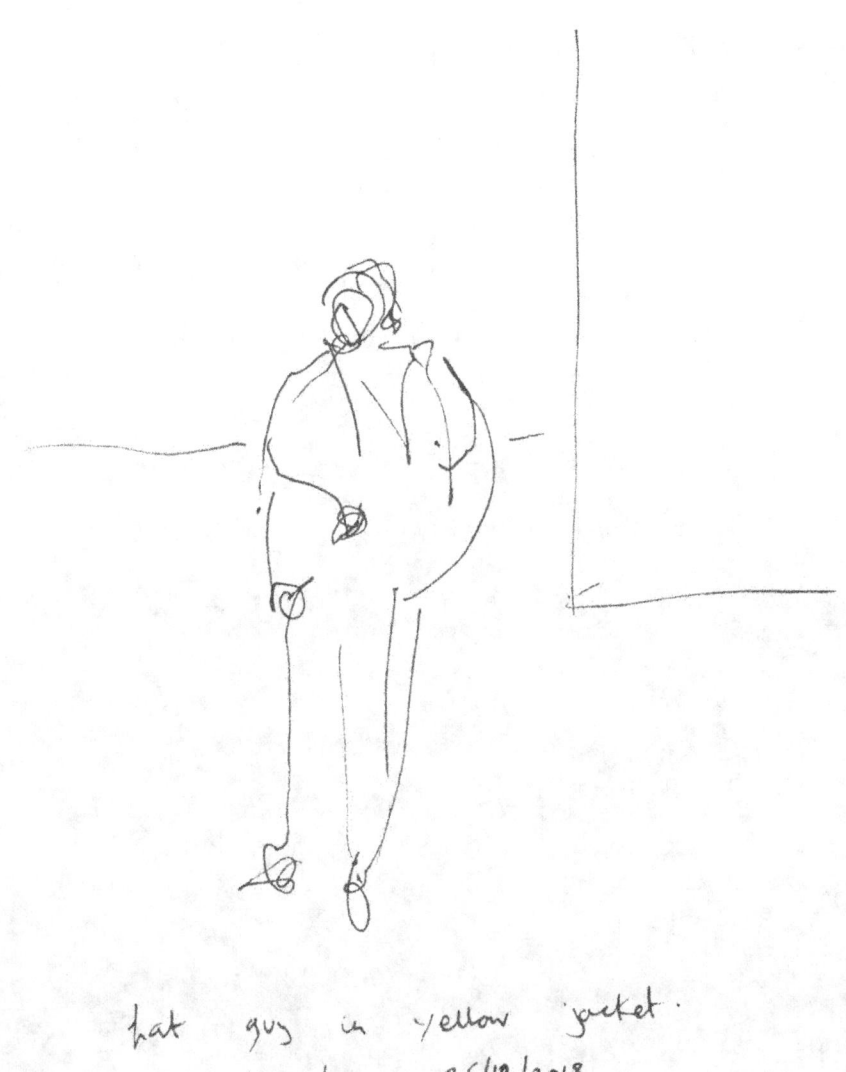

hat guy in yellow jacket.
Haarlem 26/12/2018

Lady checking her phone, Haarlem, 2018, ink on paper, 21 x 29.7 cm

Dame schaut auf ihr Handy, Haarlem, 2018, Tinte auf Papier, 21 x 29,7 cm

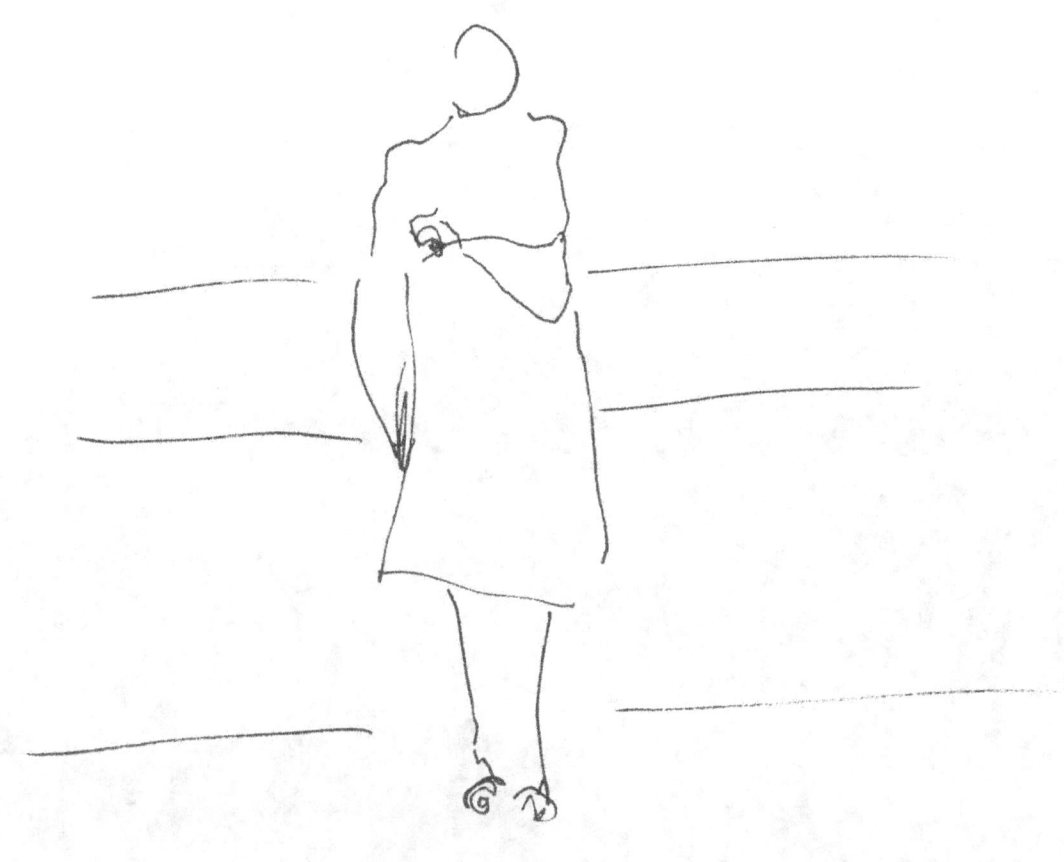

lady checks her phone
Haarlem 26/12/2018

Woman smoking, Haarlem, 2018, ink on paper, 21 x 29.7 cm

Frau raucht, Haarlem, 2018, Tinte auf Papier, 21 x 29,7 cm

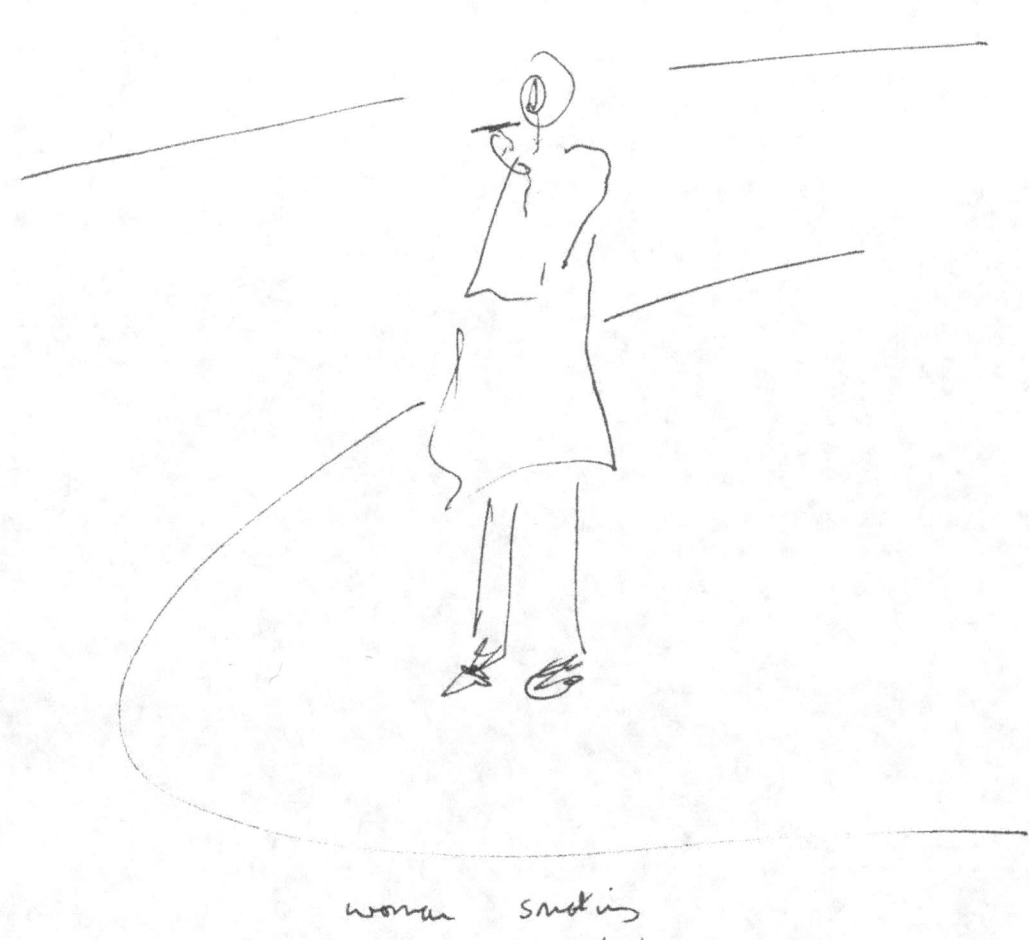

woman smoking
Haarlem   26/12/2018

Man with bowtie, Haarlem, 2018, ink on paper,
21 x 29.7 cm

Mann mit Fliege, Haarlem, 2018, Tinte auf Papier,
21 x 29,7 cm

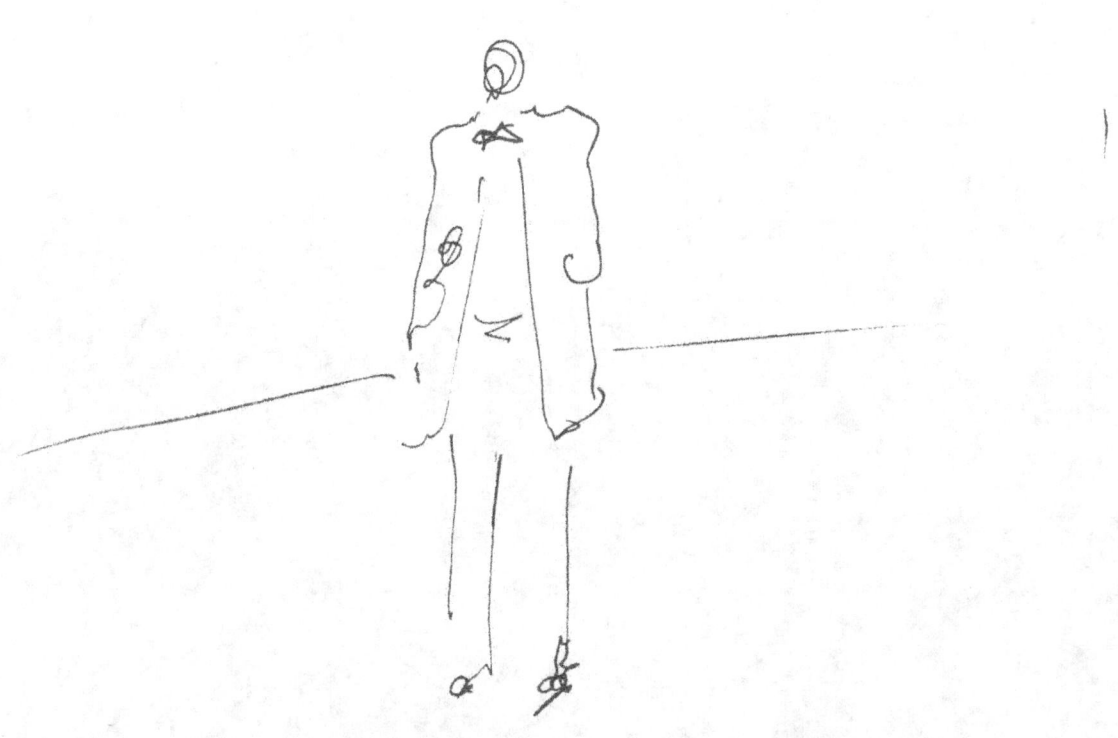

man with bowtie
Haarlem 26/12/2018

Group of people, Haarlem, 2018, ink on paper, 21 x 29.7 cm

Gruppe von Menschen, Haarlem, 2018, Tinte auf Papier, 21 x 29,7 cm

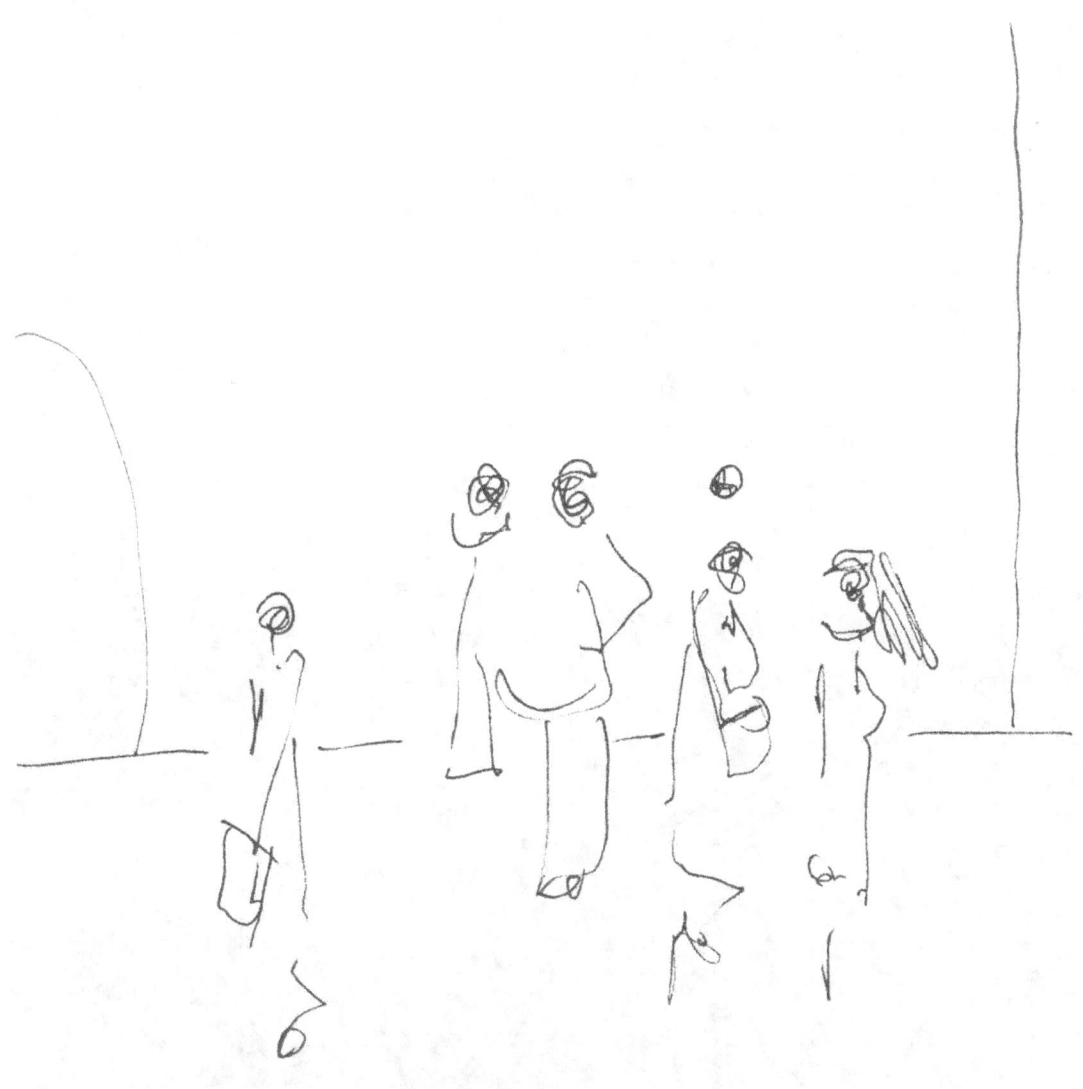

group of people
Haarlem 26/12/2018

Man with headphones and baseball cap,
Haarlem, 2018, ink on paper, 21 x 29.7 cm

Mann mit Kopfhörer und Baseballmütze, Haarlem,
2018, Tinte auf Papier, 21 x 29,7 cm

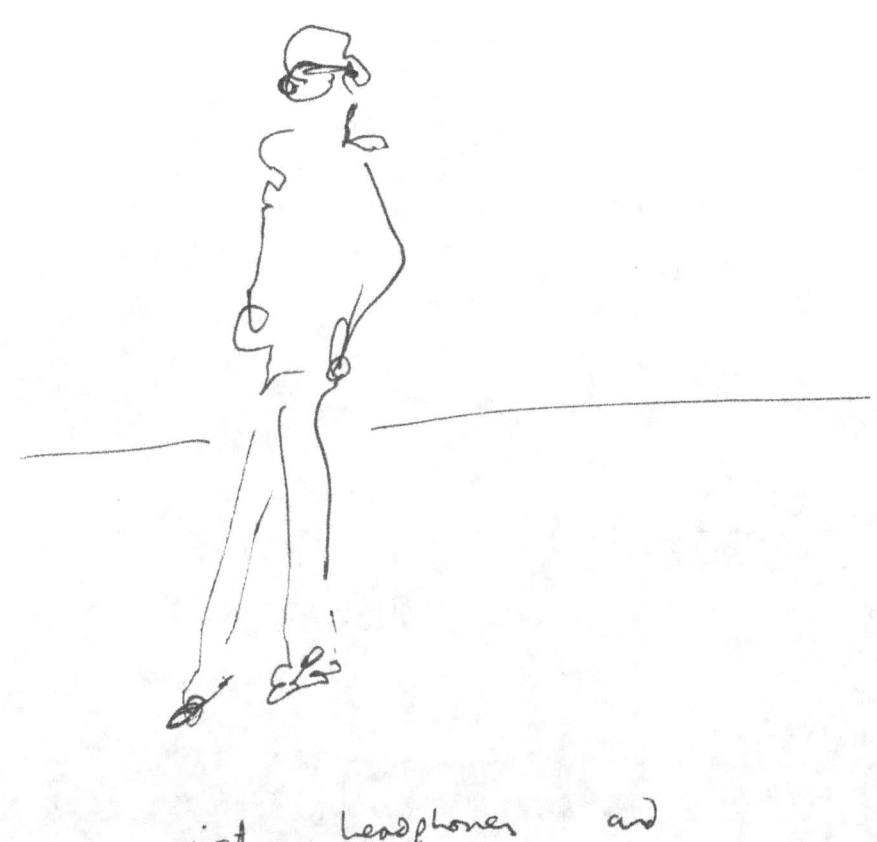

man with headphones and
baseball cap. Haarlem
26/12/2018

Man with his hands behind his back, Haarlem,
2018, ink on paper, 21 x 29.7 cm

Mann mit den Händen hinter seinem Rücken,
Haarlem, 2018, Tinte auf Papier, 21 x 29,7 cm

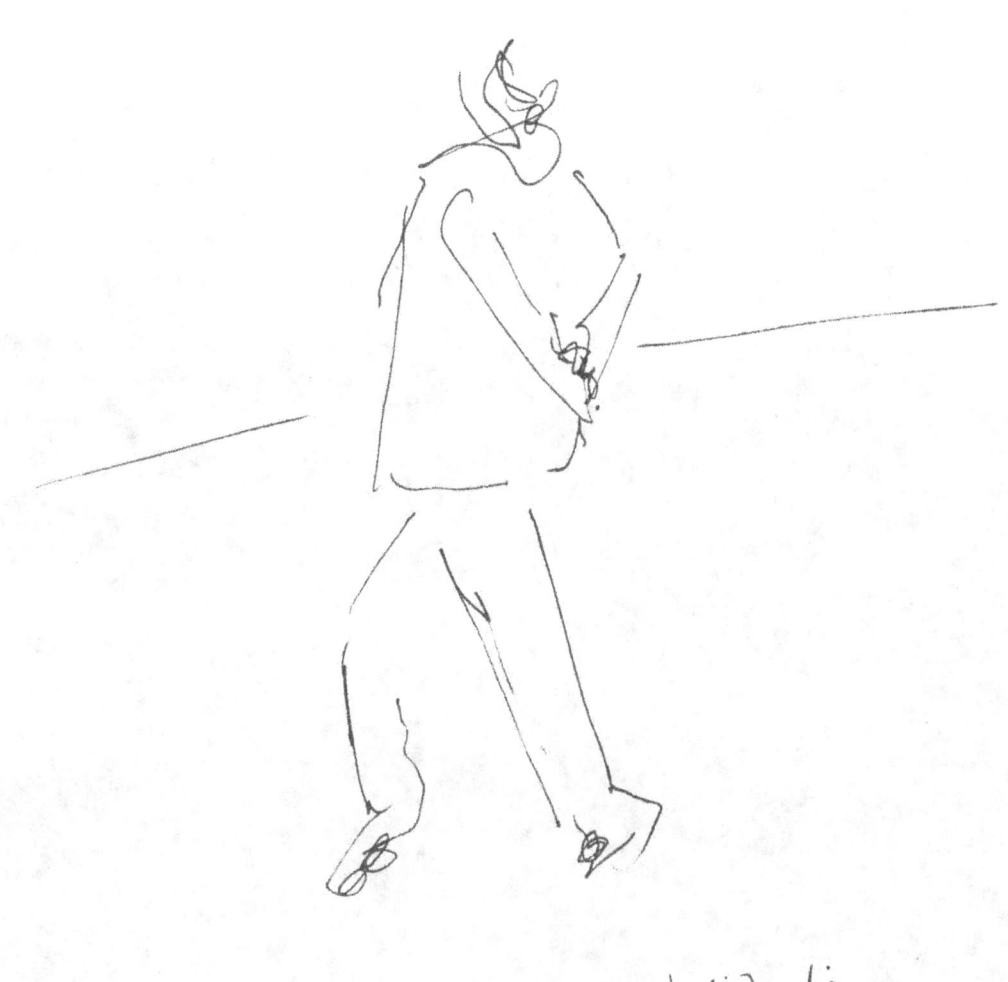

man with his hands behind his
back. Haarlem 26/12/2018

Woman in a hood, Haarlem, 2018, ink on paper,
21 x 29.7 cm

Frau mit Kapuze, Haarlem, 2018, Tinte auf Papier,
21 x 29,7 cm

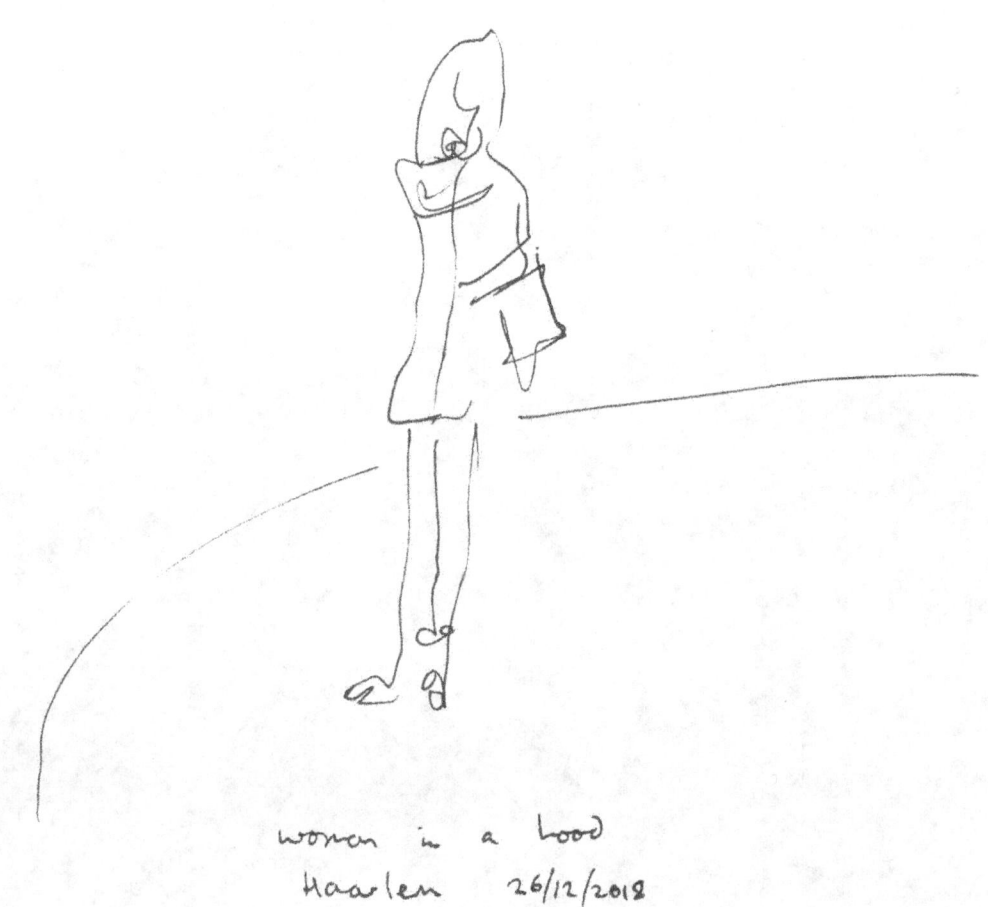

woman in a hood
Haarlem 26/12/2018

Couple, Haarlem, 2018, ink on paper, 21 x 29.7 cm   *Paar*, Haarlem, 2018, Tinte auf Papier, 21 x 29,7 cm

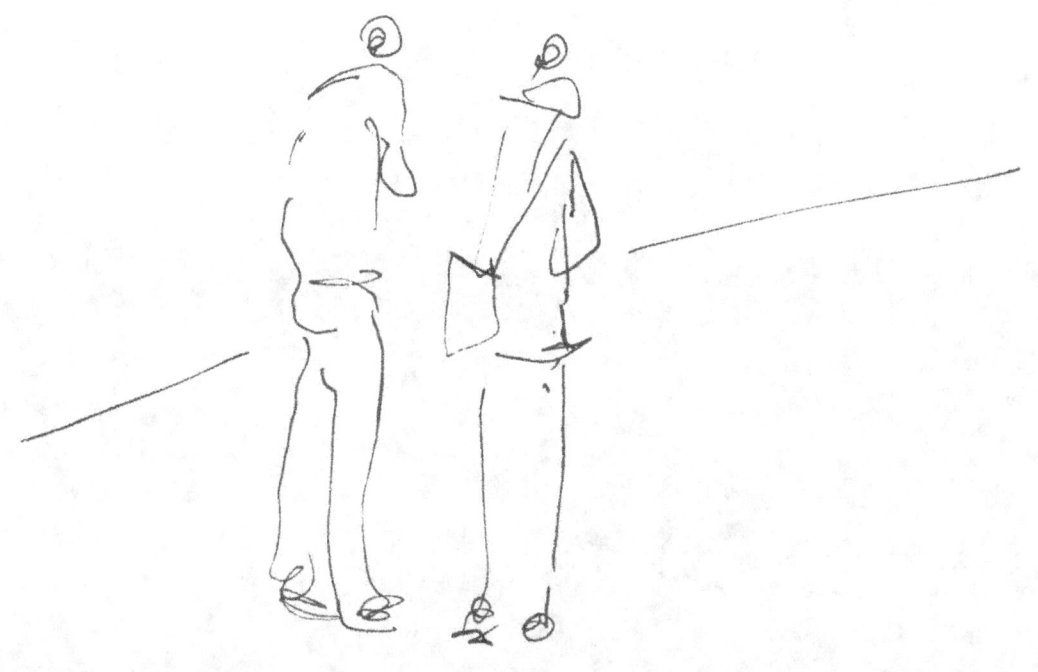

Couple . Haarlem 26/12/2018

Woman with bunch of flowers, Haarlem, 2018, ink
on paper, 21 x 29.7 cm

Frau mit Blumenstrauß, Haarlem, 2018, Tinte auf
Papier, 21 x 29,7 cm

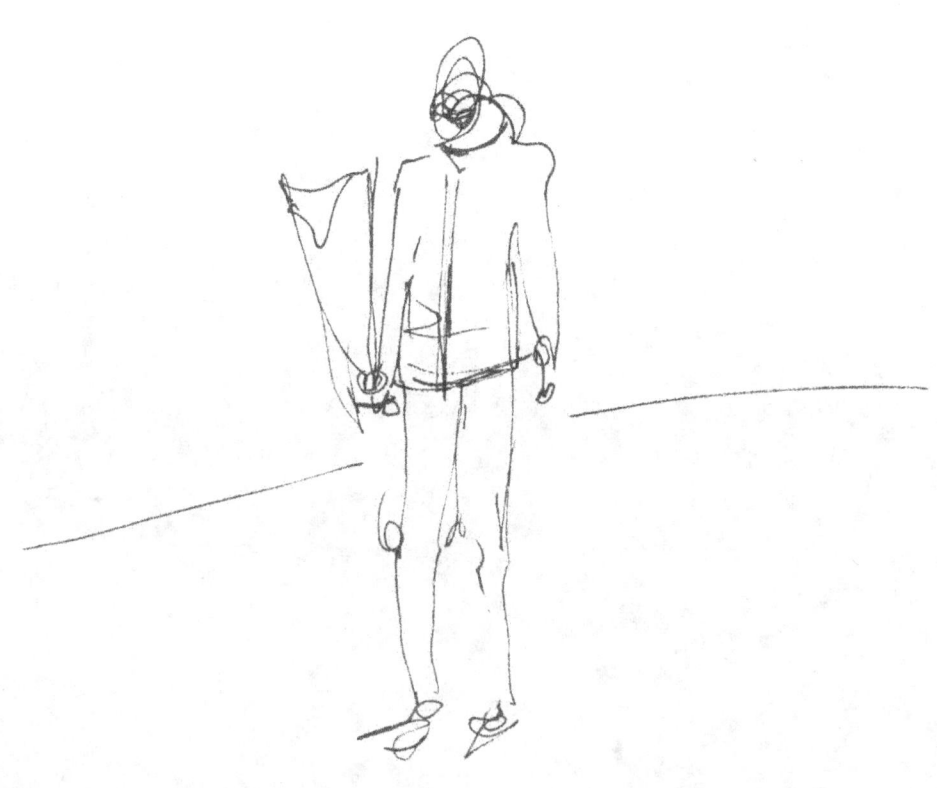

woman with bunch of
flowers. Haarlem 26/12/2018

Old couple, Haarlem, 2018, ink on paper,
21 x 29.7 cm

Älteres Paar, Haarlem, 2018, Tinte auf Papier,
21 x 29,7 cm

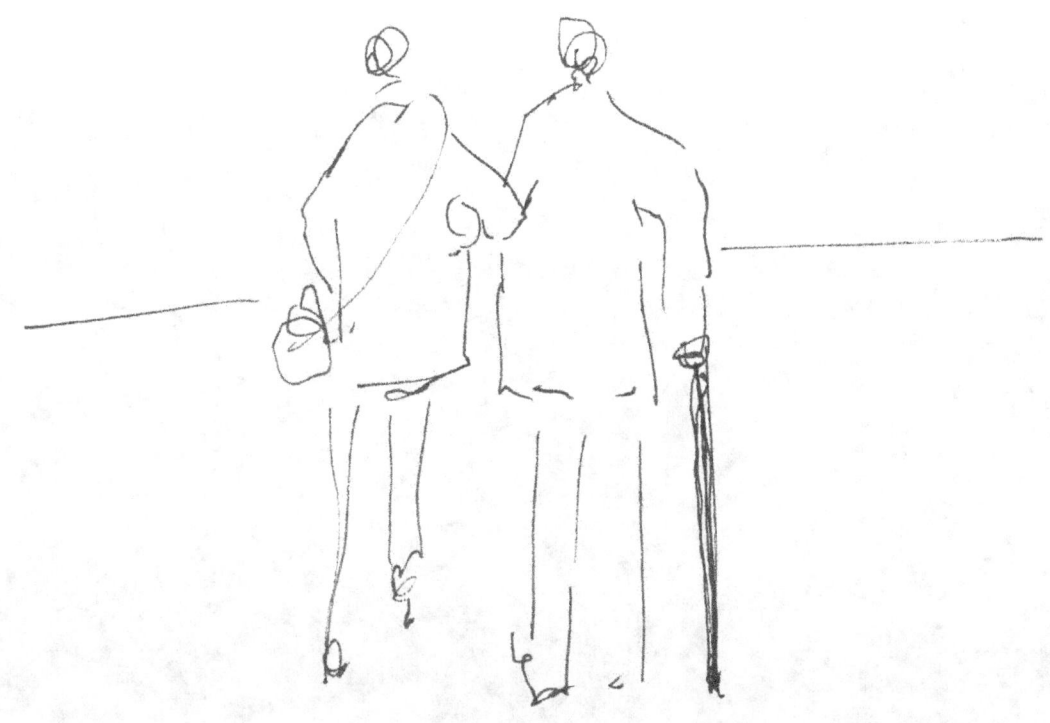

old couple. Haarlem 26/12/2018

Smoking man, Haarlem, 2018, ink on paper, 21 x 29.7 cm

Rauchender Mann, Haarlem, 2018, Tinte auf Papier, 21 x 29,7 cm

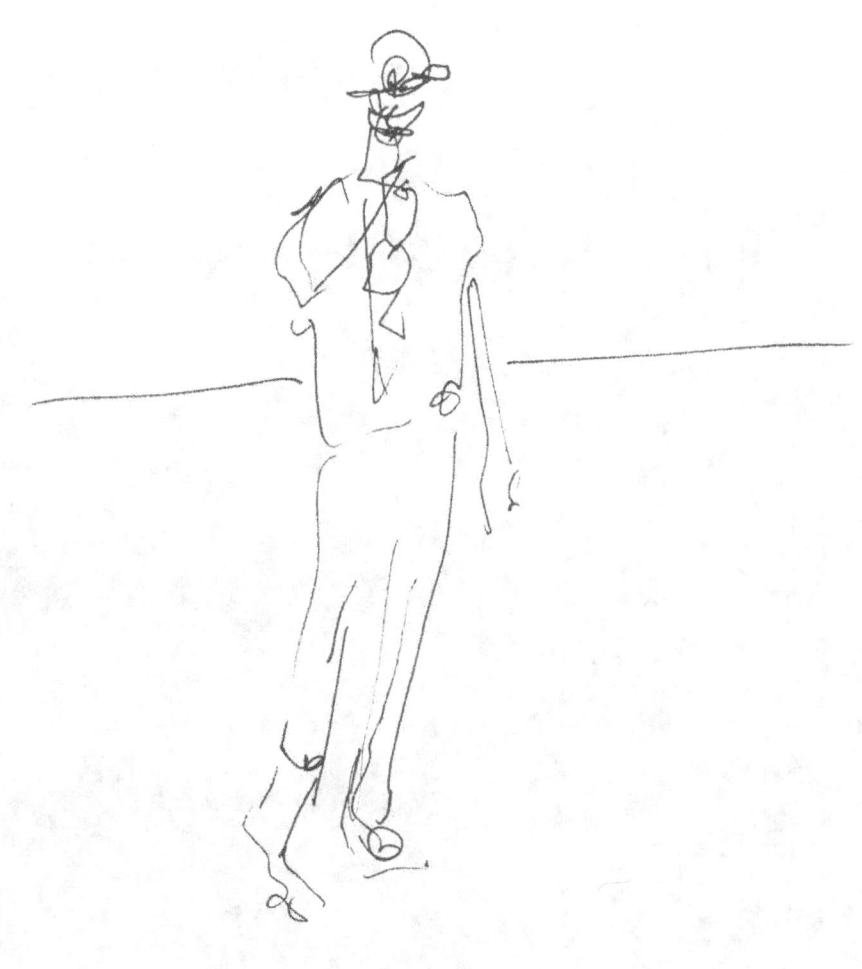

Smoking man
Haarlem 26/12/2018

Woman with large yellow scarf, Haarlem, 2018, ink
on paper, 21 x 29.7 cm

Frau mit großem gelbem Schal, Haarlem, 2018,
Tinte auf Papier, 21 x 29,7 cm

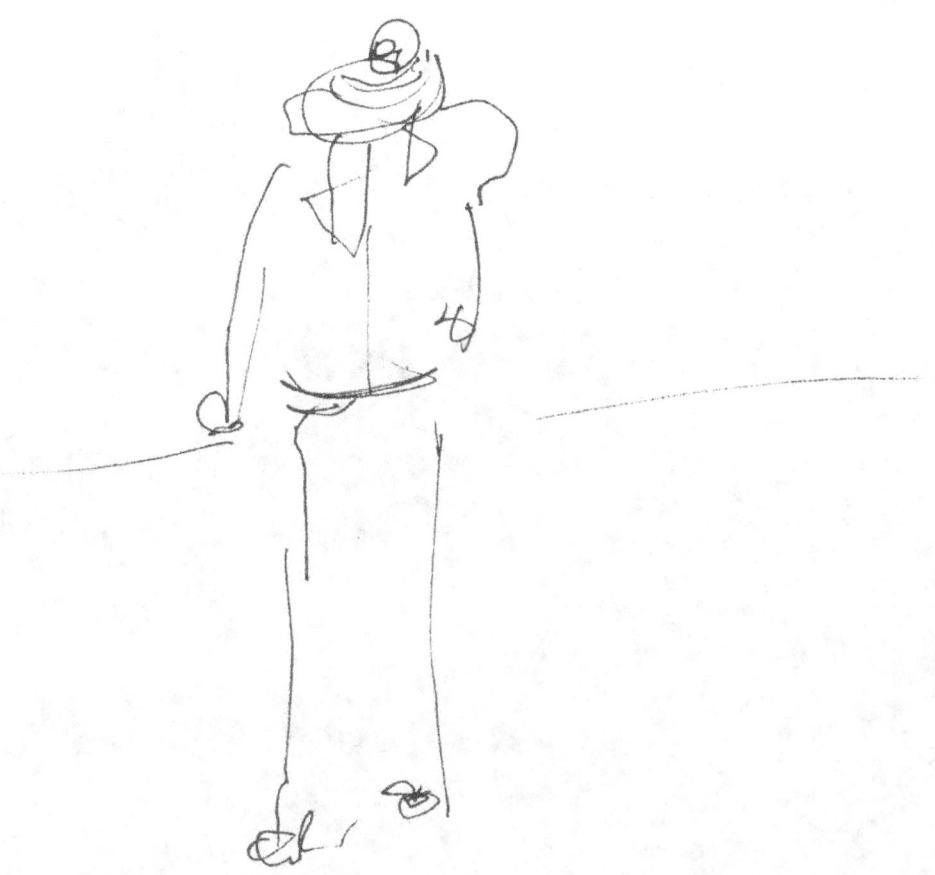

woman with large yellow
scarf. Haarlem 26/12/2018

Pointing man, Haarlem, 2018, ink on paper, 21 x 29.7 cm

Mann deutet auf etwas, Haarlem, 2018, Tinte auf Papier, 21 x 29,7 cm

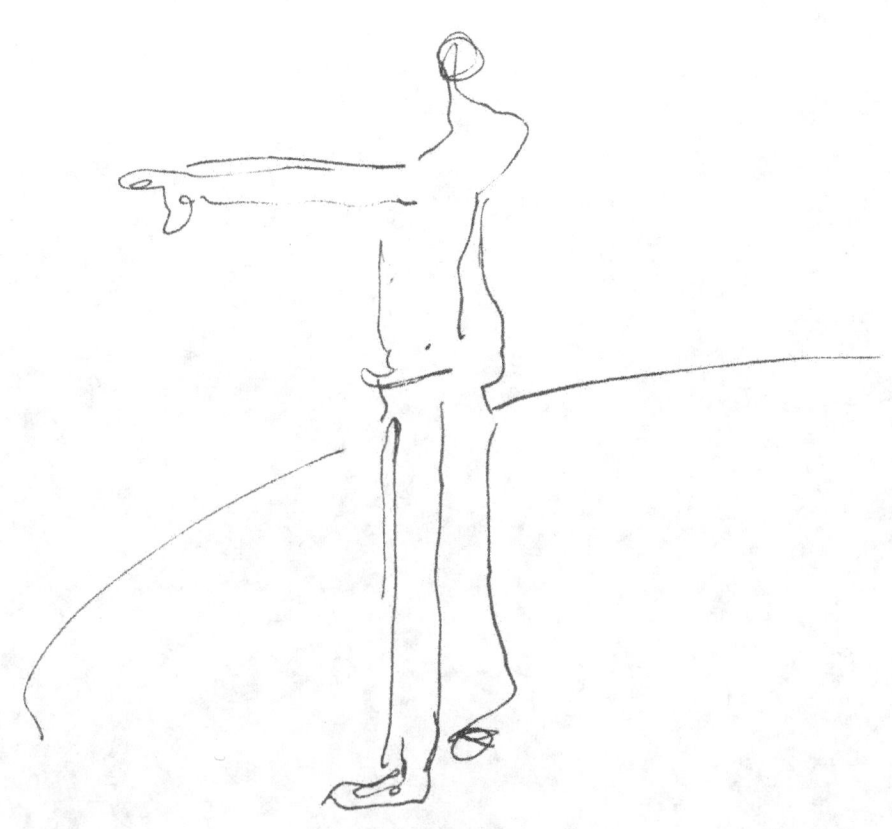

pointing man.
Haarlem 26/12/2018

Woman with red hat, Haarlem, 2018, ink on paper, 21 x 29.7 cm

Frau mit rotem Hut, Haarlem, 2018, Tinte auf Papier, 21 x 29,7 cm

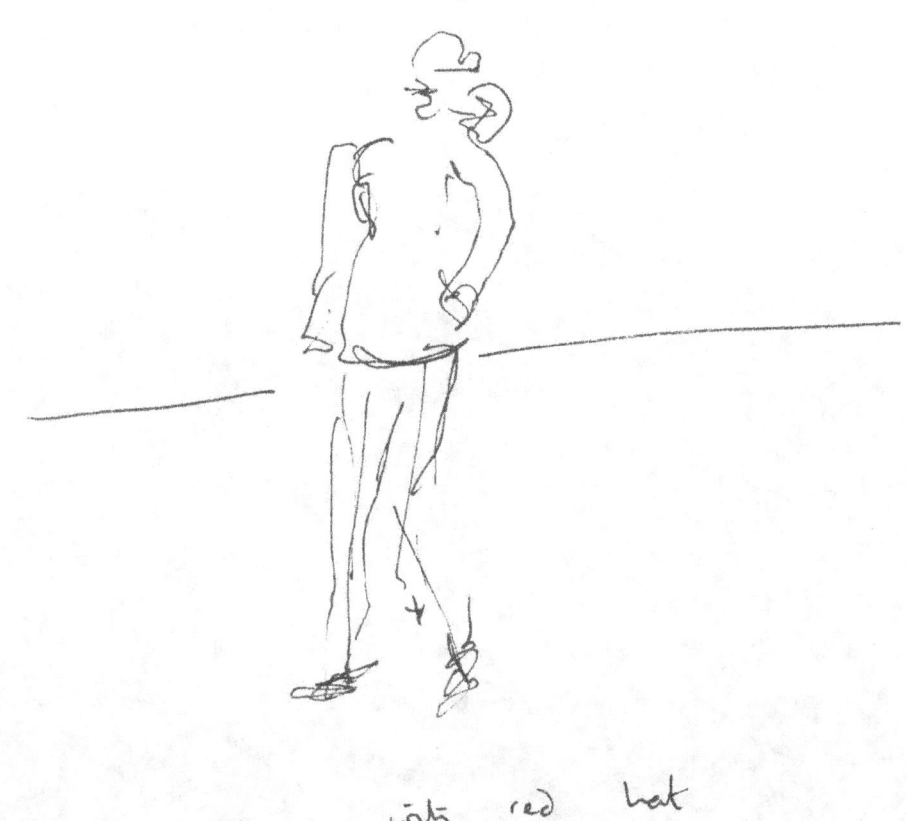

woman with red hat
Haarlem.   26/12/2018

Father and son, Haarlem, 2018, ink on paper,
21 x 29.7 cm

Vater und Sohn, Haarlem, 2018, Tinte auf Papier,
21 x 29,7 cm

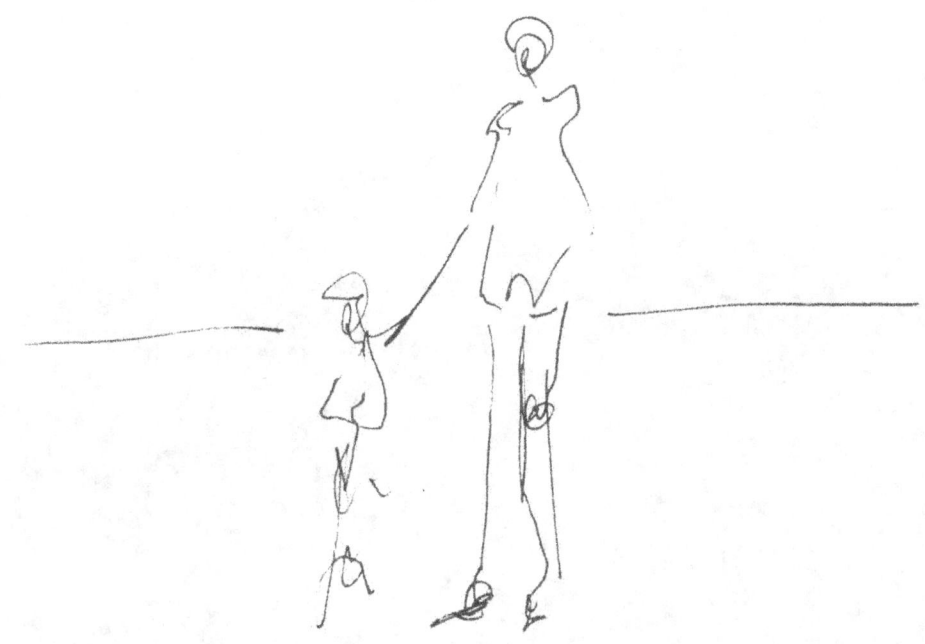

father and son
Haarlem. 26/12/2018

Biography

Kate Pelling is best known for video works using direct address to camera and artist's books consisting of drawings that examine editing processes. In 2012, she founded Fifth Floor Publications, which is a platform that publishes artists' books that use transdisciplinary methods, with an emphasis on experimental works that examine aspects of making artists' film and video and/or drawing practices. In 2013, Pelling relocated from London, UK, to Niederbrechen, a small town in Hessen, Germany. Since then, her work has focussed on transdisciplinary approaches to drawing and collaborative practice. In 2016, she completed her PhD at Chelsea College of Arts, London, titled *Select Reject Reconfigure: Editing Speech in Artists' Direct Address to Camera* which used drawing as a strategy for editing video. Pelling has exhibited extensively in the UK and the USA, she had a retrospective at the Shortini International Film Festival, Augusta, Italy (2011) and a solo exhibition at The Idea Store Whitechapel (2014), and she has also exhibited in Bulgaria, Canada, Germany, Lithuania, Portugal, and Switzerland. Publications include *Bearbeitungsklappe [Editing Flap]* (2016), *[Video] Klappe* (2014) and *A Relational [Video] Grammar: Extrapolation* (2013), all published by Fifth Floor Publications.

Biografie

Kate Pelling ist vor allem für ihre Videos, in denen sie die Kamera direkt einsetzt, und für ihre Kunstbücher mit Zeichnungen, die Editionsprozesse untersuchen, bekannt. 2012 gründete sie den Verlag Fifth Floor Publications, eine Plattform zur Veröffentlichung der Bücher von Künstlern, die transdisziplinäre Methoden anwenden und experimentellen Werken, die den Aspekten des Filmens, der Videoaufnahme und der Zeichnung besondere Bedeutung beimessen. 2013 zog Kate Pelling von London nach Deutschland, in die kleine hessische Stadt Niederbrechen. Seitdem liegt der Schwerpunkt ihrer Arbeit auf transdisziplinären Ansätzen im Hinblick auf Zeichnen und Kollaboration. 2016 erreichte sie am Chelsea College of Arts in London den Doktorgrad mit ihrem Werk *Select Reject Reconfigure: Editing Speech in Artists' Direct Address to Camera*, in dem sie Zeichnen als eine Strategie zur Edition von Videos anwendete. Viele ihre Werke waren mehrfach auf Ausstellungen in Großbritannien und den USA zu sehen, 2011 hatte sie eine Retrospektive beim Shortini International Film Festival, Augusta in Italien, 2014 eine Soloaustellung bei The Idea Store Whitechapel. Auch in Bulgarien, Kanada, Deutschland, Litauen, Portugal und der Schweiz waren ihre Werke zu sehen. Unter ihren Veröffentlichungen sind *Bearbeitungsklappe [Editing Flap]*, 2016, *[Video] Klappe*, 2014, und *A Relational [Video] Grammar: Extrapolation*, 2013, alle veröffentlicht bei Fifth Floor Publications.

Acknowledgements

This book has been a bit of a labour of love over the last two years. It appears to be a very simple concept but a lot of work was involved in getting to this point and so there are many people to thank.

I would like to express my sincere thanks to all of those who support me and my work on a regular basis, Nathan Evans, Paul Ryan, Otelo Fabião, Hazel Pelling, Christina März, Claudia Schicktanz, Britta Färber, Jim Irvin's voice, Antje Meißner and Martin Hönes.

I would like to thank the Singel Hotel in Amsterdam for putting me in an attic room, it was a claustrophobic little room and provided very little opportunity to stand up.

I am very grateful to Martijn Zegel at Teylers Museum, Haarlem, for his kind permission to use the image *Goltzius's Right Hand* (1588).

I would like to thank Martin Peter for translating all of the text into German, and Antje Meißner and Paul Ryan for proof reading so thoroughly.

Last but definitely not least, but I would like to posthumously thank Hendrick Goltzius for providing a context for this book. His work sparked an interest in me, and a desire to talk about it, and the results of that moment are now here for everyone to enjoy.

As always, and particularly due to the themes that run through this work, this publication is dedicated to the memory

Danksagungen

Das vorliegende Buch ist im Laufe der vergangenen zwei Jahre vor allem aus Liebe zum Thema entstanden. Auf den ersten Blick scheint das Konzept recht einfach, doch war sehr viel Arbeit erforderlich, um so weit zu kommen. Es gibt also viele Menschen, denen ich danken möchte.

All jenen, die mich und meine Arbeit regelmäßig unterstützen, möchte ich meinen aufrichtigen Dank aussprechen: Nathan Evans, Paul Ryan, Otelo Fabiao, Hazel Pelling, Christina März, Claudia Schicktanz, Britta Färber, der Stimme von Jim Irvin, Antje Meißner und Martin Hönes.

Vielen Dank an das Singel Hotel in Amsterdam, wo ich in einem kleinen Zimmer ganz oben untergebracht wurde, das so beengt war, dass es Platzangst hervorrief und es kaum möglich war, aufzustehen.

Sehr dankbar bin ich Martijn Zegel vom Teylers Museum in Haarlem für die freundliche Genehmigung der Verwendung der Darstellung von Goltzius' rechter Hand (1588).

Ich möchte Martin Peter für die Übersetzung des Textes dieses Buches ins Deutsche und Antje Meißner und Paul Ryan für das Korrekturlesen danken.

Nicht zuletzt möchte ich Hendrick Goltzius posthum dafür danken, dass er den Kontext für dieses Buch geschaffen hat. Sein Werk weckte mein Interesse

of my brothers, John and Stuart Pelling.

und den Wunsch, mich darüber auszutauschen. Das Resultat liegt nun vor und jeder kann sich daran erfreuen.

Wie immer, und ganz besonders auf Grund der Thematik des vorliegenden Buches, ist dieses Werk dem Andenken meiner Brüder John und Stuart Pelling gewidmet.

Fifth Floor Publications

Fifth Floor Publications was founded
in 2012 and is based in London, UK
and Frankfurt am Main, Germany. Fifth
Floor Publications is a publisher of
artists' books that use transdisciplinary
methods, with an emphasis on
experimental works that examine
aspects of making artists' film and video
or drawing practices.

Previously published titles include
*A Relational [Video] Grammar:
Extrapolation* by Kate Pelling (2013),
[Video] Klappe by Kate Pelling (2014)
and *Bearbeitungsklappe [Editing Flap]*
by Kate Pelling (2016).

Fifth Floor Publications

Fifth Floor Publications wurde im
Jahre 2012 gegründet und hat ihren
Sitz in London, Großbritannien und
Frankfurt am Main, Deutschland.
Fifth Floor Publications ist ein
Verlag für Künstlerbücher, die
transdisziplinäre Methoden einsetzen,
mit Schwerpunkt auf experimentellen
Werken, die Aspekte der Schaffung
von Künstlerfilmen, Video und
Zeichnungspraktiken untersuchen.

Unter den bereits veröffentlichten Titeln
sind A Relational [Video] Grammar:
Extrapolation von Kate Pelling (2013),
[Video] Klappe von Kate Pelling (2014)
und *Bearbeitungsklappe [Editing Flap]*
von Kate Pelling (2016).

www.ingramcontent.com/pod-product-compliance
Lightning Source LLC
Chambersburg PA
CBHW080933170526
45158CB00008B/2273

* 9 7 8 0 9 5 7 6 1 2 8 3 9 *